WHERE HAVE ALL THE
IRISH GONE?

WHERE HAVE ALL THE
IRISH GONE?
THE SAD DEMISE OF IRELAND'S ONCE
RELEVANT FOOTBALLERS

KEVIN O'NEILL

First published by Pitch Publishing, 2017

Pitch Publishing
A2 Yeoman Gate
Yeoman Way
Worthing
Sussex
BN13 3QZ

www.pitchpublishing.co.uk
info@pitchpublishing.co.uk

A CIP catalogue record is available for this book
from the British Library.

ISBN 978-1-78531-327-1

Typesetting and origination by Pitch Publishing

Printed in the UK by TJ International, Cornwall

Contents

DEDICATION

This book is dedicated to the memory of my uncle, Thomas 'Cass' Cassidy. He took me along to my first ever Republic of Ireland international match, a 1-0 defeat against Wales in Jack Charlton's debut as manager.

Thereafter, he would take me to almost every home international and returned from countless away games with souvenirs and match programmes from each occasion including in far-flung places like Albania, Macedonia and Iran.

He loved the Irish national team and took great pride in his country's football revolution in the 1980s and beyond, and took pleasure from seeing Irishmen gain success in the English First Division (later the Premier League), whether for his favourite club side Liverpool or other teams.

Equally, for some reason he always stayed up-to-date with my writing. A quiet and dignified person, he would probably be embarrassed to be the subject of this dedication. But I will never forget his contribution to my ongoing love affair with the game and Irish football. The book is also dedicated to my children: Caelan, Jayla and Cara. Hopefully they look back on it in years to come and enjoy it or, more likely, give me a good slagging! I hope you all enjoy the read.

Thanks,
Kevin O'Neill.

Acknowledgements

I T took some time for everything to fall into place to finish this book. But for sure, it would have taken significantly longer but for the support, decency and co-operation of so many people in the last couple of years.

So, instead of reeling off a list of names who organised interviews, answered emails and put up with my incessant nagging, I genuinely thank every person who tolerated and aided me in this regard. Those who assisted will know who they are and I am grateful for their time and steadfast patience.

I would like to thank my family and friends for their support. There were times when they probably wondered if this book would ever make the shelves. Yet still, they constantly endured my latest updates and always encouraged me to keep going. Even though they never realised it, their subtle show of support was priceless, especially on days when you would question if the book would ever be published.

Eventually it was. And a few people have played key roles. I want to acknowledge the esteemed literary agent Marianne Gunn O'Connor, who was the first person in the industry to show interest in my writing, and it has been fantastic to have her on my side. Her guidance and belief in the book was an enormous boost and gave me confidence to make the book reach fruition.

Marianne was instrumental in the early stages and put me in contact with the Irish editor, Alison Walsh. Alison is an editorial genius and she helped transform the book from a somewhat scattered bunch of ideas to its present form. I learned a huge amount from Alison and will always be grateful for her assistance and expertise.

I also want to thank Mark Godfrey, the editor of *The Football Pink* website and magazine. Mark gave me the opportunity to contribute to his forums in the last 18 months and, although not directly involved in the book, did provide me with a confidence boost when I wasn't too sure where my writing career was going. I also want to thank the various media and broadcast outlets who promoted the book and everyone who sent well-wishes and words of encouragement when I first announced, publicly, that the book had been accepted for publication.

Of course, there would be no book without Pitch Publishing, a most wonderful and leading independent sports book publisher. For years they have given sports writers – both aspiring and established – the opportunity to tell their story, and Jane and Paul Camillin must take the plaudits for doing so. I am grateful for their interest in the book and to everyone associated with Pitch Publishing who helped in the project.

Of course, I also want to thank every football player interviewed in the book. Without their co-operation and ability to openly speak about their experiences in English football then this book could not have happened, so thanks very much to each and every one of you.

I really hope that you, the reader, can sit back, relax and enjoy the book. And thank you so much for your interest, which means a great deal and might just encourage me to get stuck into another one in the near future.

Thank you so much,

Kevin O'Neill.

You can contact the author by email at kevoneill2@yahoo.com or on Twitter @kevoneillwriter

Introduction

THE Irish soccer team has specialised in moral victories for quite some time. The latest of these 'victories' came at the 2016 European Championships in France when the Boys in Green qualified out of their group to reach the last 16 knockout stage.

There, the Irish team was eliminated by the host nation. But their heartening endeavour in that match and, indeed, in the final group match victory against Italy, which ensured they made it to the knockouts, won much praise from the thousands of Irish supporters who made the journey to France. As well, most media commentators were fairly fulsome in their praise of Ireland's efforts throughout the tournament, apart from when a star-studded Belgian side brushed them aside in the second group match.

The Irish side undoubtedly left its mark on the tournament with the Dublin midfield duo of Robbie Brady and Jeff Hendrick particularly catching the eye. But in many ways, therein lies the problem facing Ireland in this day and age. For despite Hendrick's all-action and confident displays and Brady's momentous goal against the Italians, both players began the Championships attached to clubs in the second tier of England's professional leagues.

And for Irish football fans, what you are about to read is far removed from the beautiful fairytale memory of Brady's wonderful diving header against the Azzurri.

Instead, *Where Have all the Irish Gone?* is a hard-hitting, factual account of what has happened to Irish footballers in top-class English league football over the past 20years.

In this book, I will find out how and why the fortunes of Irish players have deteriorated so dramatically – and quickly – while also recalling better times, when the Irish triumphed in England with great regularity. In a series of face-to-face interviews with fresh talent, I will look at how young Irish players fend for themselves in the cutthroat world of English academy football, and consider those who have fallen by the wayside in doing so. Crucially, I'll also discover if there is light at the end of the tunnel for Irish football, by taking a look into the future for Irish players in England, and for future generations in the Irish schoolboy system. In doing so, I'll be talking to key players in the game, from the footballers themselves, to the managers, and to former icons of the Irish game.

Put simply, Irish players are no longer relevant at the top of English football, usually playing for unglamorous clubs in unglamorous places. They know Oxford and Oldham but not Old Trafford, and they know the way to Accrington, not Anfield.

Although close to 200,000 Irish football fans, men and women, board flights annually to England for Premier

League matches, it is some time since they saw 'one of their own' starring in a leading side.

Can you think of the last one? Roy Keane? And he retired almost a decade ago.

To emphasise the point, Seamus Coleman is currently seen as the jewel in the Irish crown, after his selection on the Premier League Team of the Year in 2014.

But Coleman plays for Everton, who despite an illustrious past have been left behind in the modern era and have failed to win a trophy for 20 years.

No longer do we see Liam Brady, Denis Irwin, Paul McGrath and countless others of their ilk proudly showcase the best of Irish talent on the biggest stage.

And the glorious clubs, the major institutions of Arsenal, Liverpool and Manchester United, are no longer represented in Irish international squads.

Indeed, if the Ireland manager wants to run the rule over players ahead of an international, he has no business at any of the Premier League's outstanding fixtures.

The goings-on at Arsenal, Chelsea, Liverpool and the two Manchester giants are insignificant to the Irish cause, so instead, he is better served casting his eye over Burnley against Stoke or some other of the Premier League's middle to lower class teams; or even at an English Championship (second tier) game, a level at which almost one-third of senior Irish players competed by 2015.

It's clear that all is not well in Irish football, but why?

At the heart of the decline lies money, pressure and a gargantuan increase in the level of competition faced by Irish players in England's academy system.

First-team managers are under intense pressure to perform, week in, week out. The pressure to accumulate league points is relentless, because every Premier League placing is worth more and more money. Clubs don't have time to wait for results, and the few managers that insist on giving youth its chance tend to be sacked before too long. In modern times, the one notable exception to the norm was the emergence of a raft of high-class players from Manchester United's Academy to play successfully for the Red Devils for a number of years. Dubbed 'Fergie's Fledglings', in reference to their manager Sir Alex Ferguson, the players involved were of supreme quality, most notably David Beckham, Nicky Butt, Ryan Giggs, the Neville brothers and Paul Scholes. Undoubtedly, their introduction to United's first team, and their continuing presence in the side for a decade, required Ferguson to show guts and plenty of trust in his young stars, but not many managers have followed his example since. It is also noteworthy though that Ferguson, while never shy of giving youth a chance, also felt a need, from about 1996 onwards, to look further afield for new talent. For example, between the years 1996 and the year of his retirement, 2013, Ferguson signed 76 players, of which 56 were non-British / Irish, indicating that even the most successful manager in English football history felt it necessary to keep up with the times when Premier League clubs discovered new-found riches.

In 2014, the difference, financially, between finishing first and bottom in the Premier League was over £30 million, and that was before calculating the vast sums earned through massive television deals.

When faced with such over-burdening pressure, managers naturally err on the side of caution, as they bid to protect their jobs. They rely on older, more experienced players to see them through, and if a new player is required, the answer is usually drawn from the club chequebook – not from within.

The academy system, in England, is one of the game's great contradictions. For despite enormous investments made by clubs each year to embellish academy facilities, the majority of English clubs fail miserably when it comes to giving first-team opportunities to young players.

In late 2014, for example, Manchester City opened a state-of-the-art football academy costing £200m, an academy rated as arguably the best and most modern in Europe. Yet, since City was subject to a massive financial takeover in 2008, not one English or Irish player developed exclusively by the club has started a match in the Premier League. They are not alone in that sense, as the chase for glory, domestically and abroad, sees the major English clubs turn their noses up at Irish players.

Some observers might call these 'excuses', rather than 'reasons', for why Irish players no longer dine at the top table. They argue that Irish players are simply not as good as before, and that they fall dismally short when compared to those playing for England's top sides. Such a theory is pretty straightforward and strikes hard to the heart of those connected to the Irish game, but this blunt assessment cannot be dismissed.

Nowadays, a young player might be the best in Dublin, or Cork or Waterford. They might be a certainty for the various underage international sides, and they might be idolised locally, from an early age, for possessing superior skill to their peers, but when they get to England, it's a whole new world, and it's not always one they enjoy.

Regularly, they lack the physical prowess and technical skill of their new academy colleagues. This owes itself, primarily, to a lack of exposure to organised and efficient ways of training in Ireland.

So, as soon as an Irish player arrives in England, they are playing catch-up. And what's more, they are not merely competing with the best young players from England, Northern Ireland, Scotland and Wales. Far from it: they are up against players from every corner of the globe, which further inhibits their chance to become top Premier League players.

The travelling hordes to England have generally been infatuated by English football from an early age. They want to see the stars of the game. They yearn to be part of it, and are hellbent on seeing Sergio Agüero, Cesc Fabregas, Eden Hazard and Wayne Rooney. But they are damned if they think they will see Irish players gracing Anfield, Old Trafford or Stamford Bridge – unless in the colours of visiting mid-table sides.

Back in Ireland, where a poorly attended, inadequately funded League of Ireland acts as the ugly sister to the English game, their attention is deflected by a deluge of top-class English matches, beamed to their homes on an almost bi-daily basis, by a myriad of different broadcasters.

Is it any wonder that they have no desire to stand among a few hundred hardy souls in less than opulent surroundings, watching a local match?

And when the figurehead of the Football Association of Ireland (FAI), John Delaney, describes the domestic league as 'a difficult child', as he did in October 2014, you have a really big problem.

Aside from that, the domestic 'product', if you like, and its largely part-time ethos, dictates that the League of Ireland simply cannot live with its English counterpart. And then there is a schoolboy system in place, in Ireland, that is as complex as it is non-productive.

The masses will always flock to the English alternative, and the same applies for young Irish players keen to take their skill to a more professional environment. The potential rewards of 'making it' – both professionally and personally – are almost ludicrous.

As Noel King, the Ireland Under-21 manager puts it, for an Irish youngster to succeed in the Premier League they must prove they are worth in the region of £30 million. For almost all Irish players going to England, generally in their mid-teens, proving such is well beyond their actual ability, hence England has become nothing more than a land of broken dreams for aspiring Irish players.

In this book, I will take an in-depth look at the Irish question, looking at everything from the training of young Irish players to the challenges they face in the highly competitive world of English academy football. I will also look at the great Irish players of the past and consider whether, one day, the country might be positioned to again dine at the top table of English football, having, for the past few decades, fed off scraps to just about keep it alive.

Chapter 1

The Demise

AS a teenager, Thomas Morgan, from inner-city Dublin, had Sir Alex Ferguson in his living room, trying to persuade the 15-year-old midfielder to abandon his plans to join Blackburn Rovers. They were emerging as title rivals to Ferguson's Manchester United and he was keen for Morgan to move to Old Trafford.

Morgan chose Blackburn, signing for the Ewood Park side in 1994. A year later, Blackburn won their one and only Premier League title. But despite training with the league-winning squad, and making the bench for league and European matches, Morgan found himself released – and without a club – almost three years later. It was only weeks before captaining the Ireland Under-20s to a third-place finish in the 1997 World Championships in Malaysia.

Put simply, Morgan fell by the wayside as Blackburn – and their Premier League rivals – regularly shunned the promotion of youth in favour of big-money signings. The birth of the Premier League in 1992 ushered in an era of stellar signings, compounded by the Bosman ruling in 1995, which removed obstacles to foreign players playing in England – a double whammy which would change the fortunes of Irish players for ever. The fate of the class of '97 makes for salutary reading.

Morgan says, 'I chose Blackburn because they were on the way to the top. I did decent over there but circumstances and a couple of changes in manager eventually saw me let go, aged 20. I mean, I worked my socks off and made the bench in the Premier League and Champions League, but ultimately, I fell short. Every Irish player on the Malaysia trip has a story about the circumstances that dictated their career. In my case, I gave it everything but it wasn't to be. The Malaysia group wasn't full of stars, apart from Damien Duff, who was just so talented that it was obvious he would make it. When you look back, it's disappointing that only "Duffer" came through, but a few of the lads had brilliant careers in England – the likes of Robbie Ryan, who played hundreds of games for Millwall. But I think it shows just how hard it is in England.'

Morgan, who went for trials with Blackpool, Coventry City and Rochdale before returning to Ireland with St Patrick's Athletic, was captain of a barely fancied Irish squad – of which 16 were contracted to English clubs – that travelled to the Under-20 World Championships. Few people expected Ireland to do well and hopes were hardly raised when they lost the opening group match, against Ghana. But they responded by beating USA, 2-1, and a draw against China qualified the Irish for the last 16, where they triumphed, after extra time, against Morocco.

The Irish, managed by future senior team manager Brian Kerr, then beat a fancied Spanish side in the quarter-finals. Trevor Molloy, who spent the previous League of Ireland season with lowly Athlone Town, scored the decisive goal from the penalty spot. Molloy and defender Aidan Lynch were the only members of the squad playing in Ireland, while the Spanish side included three players – David Albelda, Miguel Angel Angulo and Gerard – that progressed to great success in La Liga with Valencia.

Ireland eventually lost to the tournament winners, Argentina, in the semi-finals, but unbowed they beat Ghana in the third-place play-off.

The players could be proud of a phenomenal achievement, but back in England they found themselves part of an English game rapidly accruing millions of pounds through increased television and sponsorship rights and gate receipts. The league had rapidly outgrown its former self. And for the top clubs, the discontinuation of UEFA's three-foreigner rule in European competitions had allowed them to cast their net far and wide, and to look towards purchasing foreign talent, often at the expense of players from England, Ireland, Scotland and Wales, from where the bulk of English football's pre-Premier League stars had once come.

Only 13 foreign players (from outside Great Britain and Ireland) took to the field on the opening weekend of the Premier League, in 1992. But by the time Morgan and his Irish colleagues were expected to impact the Premier League, at the turn of the century, players from outside Great Britain and Ireland were starting to form the bulk of each team's starting XI, with the number of foreign players participating in the Premier League, by the year 2000, reaching almost 40 per cent of the total. Additionally, many substitutes' benches in the Premier League were largely occupied by foreign players.

Their increasing presence laid down a challenge that the bulk of young Irish players would fail to meet, as the Premier League left them behind to become the richest league in Europe, a mantle held in the 1980s and early 1990s by Italy's Serie A.

The case of Dublin's Micky Cummins, a midfielder who played in all of Ireland's seven matches in Malaysia, scoring twice, was indicative of how youth team players were pushed aside in the cash-rich Premier League. Cummins had signed for Middlesbrough in the mid-1990s but they, along with Chelsea, were among the frontrunners in investing in foreign players. His arrival on Teesside coincided with the club experiencing a significant upturn in its financial fortunes, with the money generated from their promotion from the second tier backed up by heavy investment from local businessman, Steve Gibson.

The club's financial position enabled it and its famous player-manager Bryan Robson to dabble extensively in the foreign market, while also attracting established English players like Paul Gascoigne, Paul Ince, Paul Merson and Irish international Andy Townsend. Established players of their ilk were not going to be left on the sidelines in favour of promising youths.

Just before Cummins's signing, Middlesbrough also signed the Brazilian playmaker Juninho, and in the Irishman's four seasons there, which amounted to two senior appearances, Middlesbrough splashed out just under £15m in signing players for Cummins's midfield position.

He also had to compete with other fine midfielders who were at the club before his signing, including former Manchester United pair Clayton Blackmore and Bryan Robson. Middlesbrough's overseas recruitment soon went into overdrive, as Italian striker Fabrizio Ravanelli arrived for a club record £7m. Other foreign stars, like Brazilians Branco and Emerson (a midfielder) and Danish striker Mikkel Beck, soon pitched up at Boro, as they and other Premier League clubs spent lavishly – and often.

The Premier League's hunt for the world's best players eventually led to Chelsea becoming the first English club to field an all-foreign starting XI in the Premier League, in a 1999 fixture against Southampton. Ten years later, Arsenal became the first to name an all-foreign matchday squad in the Premier League (then 16 players), and by that point the average number of foreign players in Premier League squads stood at 13.

The top clubs, and even newly ambitious ones like Middlesbrough, were unprepared to wait for the likes of Cummins to fulfil their promise. And in 2000, Cummins eventually signed for Port Vale, playing over 250 times for the Valiants before finishing his career with Darlington, Rotherham and Grimsby Town.

Some of the most promising defenders from the 1997 Malaysia squad, namely Colin Hawkins and David Worrell, encountered similar problems at Coventry City and Blackburn Rovers respectively, both established Premier League clubs.

Worrell signed for Blackburn in 1995, just after Kenny Dalglish had led the club to the Premier League title. Blackburn were basking in the glow of the Premier League era and through the financial contributions of local businessman, Jack Walker, had become one of the country's leading forces, capable of twice breaking the English transfer record for the signings of Chris Sutton and Alan Shearer.

When Worrell signed, Blackburn had a defensive roster that had cost, in the previous three years, approximately £15m. Among those signed in that period was the Dubliner Jeff Kenna, a £1.5m investment from Southampton, while established defenders Henning Berg (who later played for Manchester United), Stéphane Henchoz (a future Liverpool player), Colin Hendry, Ian Pearce and Paul Warhurst made it extremely hard for emerging defenders to break into the Blackburn side. Frustrated and very much on the fringes, Worrell left for Dundee United in 1999 without making a single first-team appearance.

In his two seasons with Coventry, from 1995, Colin Hawkins was kept adrift of the first team by a succession of players costing over £1m, including former Liverpool player David Burrows and Irish internationals Gary Breen and Liam Daish, who had signed from Birmingham City for a combined £4m.

Meanwhile, Neale Fenn, the 1997 squad's most promising attacker, faced an almost impossible task to get into the Tottenham Hotspur side in a six-year period at White Hart Lane. Despite making his first-team debut in 1995, Fenn was never going to oust club legend Teddy Sheringham from the support striker role, a position Sheringham would occupy between 1992 and 1997, before transferring to Manchester United.

Spurs were also unafraid to spend large amounts on strikers, recruiting Chris Armstrong from Crystal Palace for a club record £4.5m in 1995. In the next two years, they signed Les Ferdinand and Steffen Iversen, both international players, for a total outlay of £8.5m. The year before Fenn departed, for Peterborough United, Spurs' spending on forwards intensified further with the £11m purchase of Serhiy Rebrov from Dynamo Kiev.

Then there was John Burns, who played alongside Morgan in the Irish midfield. He was expected to enjoy a successful career, having debuted for Nottingham Forest in 1999. Tipped to follow in the footsteps of Roy Keane, who blazed a trail for Forest before transferring to Manchester United, Burns's route to the first team was consistently blocked by a series of big-money signings and by the occupation of the midfield positions by more senior players.

He spent five years with Forest, from 1994, but managed just four first-team appearances as Forest enjoyed something of a renaissance under Frank Clark, finishing third in the 1994/95 Premier League. In Burns's time at the club, he watched, talent unfulfilled, as Forest splurged over £10m on midfielders, while the consistency of more trusted players, like Lars Bohinen and David Phillips, meant that breaking into the side was improbable. Burns finally left for Bristol City, and retired in 2005.

As if the Class of '97 didn't have enough obstacles to overcome, their efforts to fulfil their potential were not helped by the arrival of so many foreign players to England, from senior to academy/youth level, as the implications of the controversial Bosman ruling, which came into being in December 1995, hit young Irish players hard.

In essence, the ruling prevented restrictions on foreign EU players in national football leagues and permitted players within the EU to move to another club at the end of a contract without a transfer fee being paid. The case came about when Jean-Marc Bosman, a fairly unheralded Belgian midfielder, wanted to move to Dunkerque, a French side, after his contract expired at RFC Liège in 1990. Liège asked Dunkerque for a transfer fee, which the French outfit refused, and when Liège relegated Bosman to their reserve team, on reduced wages, he took his case to the courts.

In England, transfer tribunals had been used since 1981 to resolve disputes over transfer fees between clubs when transferring players at the conclusion of contracts. But the Bosman ruling made a player free to leave his club as soon as his contract expired.

The player, essentially, became all-powerful and could demand a princely signing-on fee and salary from his new club, on the basis that his new club had no transfer fee to pay.

Because clubs were permitted to play as many foreign players from within the EU as they liked, after Bosman, achievements that were improbable before the ruling became more realistic. For example, when Manchester United won a dramatic UEFA Champions League Final against Bayern Munich in 1999, only five of the 13 players that featured in the Old Trafford side could have played prior to Bosman.

Dr Raffaele Poli is the co-founder and head of the Football Observatory, a research group based in Switzerland that specialises in the demographic analysis of the football labour market. One of Dr Poli's most intriguing studies was his analysis of 'Labour Market Migration to the Five Major Leagues in European Football'. The objective of the study was to understand which leagues, clubs and players have taken advantage of the gradual opening-up of the football labour market in Europe. Drawing on statistical data from the Football Observatory, Dr Poli's study showed that the presence of foreign players in the major European leagues has increased remarkably over the last couple of decades. It also showed that the percentage of non-EU players as a cohort within the total number of foreign players has grown.

'The percentage of foreign players amongst 98 clubs in the best five European leagues (Italy, England, Spain, Germany and France) rose from 20.2 per cent in 1995/1996 to 38.6 per cent ten seasons later,' says Dr Poli.

Perhaps it's simply a question, then, of putting in place rules to limit their employment. Dr Poli, however, isn't sure that this is the right answer, unless it is accompanied by decisions to encourage the training and development of local players. He used the examples of player development in France and Switzerland as admirable models to consider for major clubs.

'The example of France, in which the presence of foreign players is the lowest and the number of local players playing abroad is the highest, shows that with a proper plan you can develop top players within Europe and not just in poor continents. The comparison between England and France shows that the presence of foreign players is not a mere consequence linked with economic reasons (the lower training costs in other continents) or the stock of human capital (the largest availability of talented young players willing to play football), but it is the result of different youth player training and development policies adopted in the last decades. The obligation of having a proper training centre in every professional French club dates back to 1973. Although this requirement was repealed in 2003 by the initiative of the top clubs, in the current economic context most of the French clubs have an interest to continue to train and develop young players in order to continue to benefit from the competitive advantage gained over the last decade.

'The Swiss case is also very interesting as it shows how the policies adopted by the football federation have improved the quality of training and developing local players. Since the late 1990s, the Swiss Football League has created a tax on transfers between domestic clubs and redistributed it amongst the clubs on the basis of youth academies' quality. Since the season 2007/08 the Swiss Football League has also rewarded clubs in the Challenge League, the second Swiss professional football division, that employ players below 21 years old and have been trained locally for at least three years in a Swiss club since the age of 15. In addition, the Swiss Football Association invests part of the national team revenues for the training and development of young players and, based on the French system, has created two pre-training academies. The good results obtained by Swiss national selections at youth level show, regardless of the presence of foreign players, that success can be partially planned. Currently, 29 footballers trained in Switzerland play in the five major European leagues, placing this small country in sixth place amongst the nations exporting football players to top elite clubs.'

So, why don't English clubs simply adopt the Swiss model? Dr Poli explains, 'It is also true that the financial strength of English clubs, the strong presence of foreign investors and the existence of global transfer networks that enrich all the main stakeholders, from players to agents to clubs, make it difficult to adopt policies similar to the French or Swiss. However, the development of appropriate youth systems are critical for the future.'

Sadly, there appears to be very few indicators that the powerful Premier League clubs are open to changing their approach to transfers and recruitment. For example, when the former English Football Association (FA) chairman, Greg Dyke, spoke (in March 2015) about a need to subdue the number of foreign players in England, Arsène Wenger, the manager of Arsenal, quickly countered by saying that players should earn the right to play in the Premier League through quality rather than their place of birth.

Mr Dyke was not the first member of English football's hierarchy to express concerns over the approach of clubs to young players. In 2007, the Professional Footballers' Association (PFA), worried about the dearth of English and home-based players breaking into Premier League sides from the academy system, published a report called 'Meltdown: The Nationality of Premier League Players and the Future of English Football'. The report provided a revealing analysis of the effect overseas players had on the English game between 1992/93 (the first Premier League season) and the 2006/07 season.

It pointed out that 498 players started Premier League matches in the 2006/07 season, of which only 191 were English, a decrease of some 47 per cent since the Premier League began. Though Irish, Scottish and Welsh players didn't figure in this particular statistic, one can undoubtedly surmise what the negative trend meant for them.

In the report, the PFA chief executive, Gordon Taylor OBE, says: 'A Premier League club can spend £2m a season on its youth system, as some do, without expecting any players to emerge from it. Having spent so much on developing young players, is it acceptable that most of the fruits of this expenditure have their path to the Premier League blocked by their clubs repeatedly buying older, ready-made players? Any good business invests in research and development. But our business has researched and developed young players – and then blocked their way to the top.'

In 2006/07, for the first time, the number of overseas players starting Premier League games overtook the number of home-grown players – that is, players from England, Northern Ireland, the Republic of Ireland, Scotland and Wales, leading Mr Taylor to describe the Premier League as 'a finishing school for the rest of the world, at the expense of our own players'.

'Nobody disputes the right of foreign players to play in England,' he says. 'On the contrary, they are some of the most welcome guests our game has ever had. They brought training and lifestyle ideas ahead of our own and broke down prejudice and national stereotypes. They set standards that have been as good for our society as they have been for our game and given tremendous pleasure to fans. But the price of the unrestricted flow of foreign players into England has been the loss of a generation of players.'

Meanwhile, new work permit rules were introduced to English football in May 2015, with the new requirements stating that non-EEA (European Economic Area) players will have to meet a minimum percentage of international matches played for their country over the previous 24-month period, as determined by that country's FIFA world ranking.

Crucially, in my opinion, the rules mean, in theory, that only the best non-EU players will be granted permission to play in England, while Premier League clubs, I suggest, must be more vigilant when considering the long-term consequences of signing a non-British / Irish player, as in the 2013/14 season, 92 of the 373 non-British / Irish players used played in fewer than ten games.

Is there really any point signing non-British / Irish players just to sit on the bench? And would it not make greater football and financial sense to allocate such 'squad' roles to players from their own academies? The FA estimates that over 30 per cent of players granted English working visas under the old system, before the introduction of the new rules in May 2015, will not succeed under the new rules, and it will be fascinating to see the reaction of the top clubs to the new regulations.

Before leaving his role as chairman of the FA in 2016, Mr Dyke had insisted that nobody wanted to stop the world's best players coming to England, such as the likes of Dennis Bergkamp, Gianfranco Zola and Patrick Vieira, but he had a desire to stall the arrival of 'bog-standard players'.

Mr Dyke, however, and indeed any individual, could never change the face of English football alone. In my opinion, the Premier League big-hitters will always be reluctant to see sweeping changes to the current status quo, while at the heart of the matter, I believe, is the fact that English football has, thus far, demonstrated little quality control in dealing with foreign and, in particular, non-EU player transfers into the country.

And that doesn't just apply to the Premier League, as by the summer of 2012, for example, 163 of the 699 players that featured in the previous season's Football League Championship (second tier) were foreign. Therefore, is it not acceptable to suggest that foreign player quotas, applicable to the three professional divisions below the Premier League, are completely necessary if players from Great Britain and Ireland are to get greater first-team opportunities in years to come?

It was not always like this though, and to understand more about the current situation, it is useful to compare it to the past, not for reasons of mere nostalgia, but to understand the roots of the current malaise.

Although the Football Association of Ireland (FAI) was not officially formed until 1921 and became affiliated to the Fédération Internationale de Football Association (FIFA) two years later, organised football in Ireland (including in the north and south) dates back to 1878, when the Belfast merchant John McAlery brought the game back to Ireland from a trip abroad. He later formed Cliftonville Football Club and they became – and remain – members of the Irish Football Association, which was founded in 1880 to oversee the organisation of football, both north and south of the border. The League of Ireland was later formed, in 1921, a few months before the formation of the FAI and following the partition of Ireland.

By then the relationship between Irish football players and English clubs had started. For example, the first recorded instance of an Irish player joining Manchester United (then called Newton Heath) occurred in 1893 when forward John Peden (Linfield, Northern Ireland) moved across the Irish Sea.

The transfer of Irish players to England for transfer fees began in the ensuing years, before Belfast Celtic's Mickey Hamill joined Manchester United in 1910 for a fee of £175.

In the early stages of the 20th century, Wexford's Bill Lacey and Elisha Scott (Belfast) also featured prominently in some of Liverpool's earliest league title wins.

For English clubs, dabbling in the Irish transfer market was a no-brainer, as the Irish came ready and relatively cheap. And their strengths were perfectly tailored to the rough and tumble of English football.

Since the conclusion of World War II in 1945, and up until recently, only Scotland had provided more players to the English leagues than Ireland; a point highlighted by Dr Patrick McGovern, a lecturer in sociology at the London School of Economics and Political Science, through his informative body of research on foreign footballers in the English leagues, 1946 to 1995.

And although English clubs now recruit from every corner of the globe, the flow of young Irish players to England has remained steady, even if most of these players never get near first-team football, and the overall trend of Irish players pursuing the dream of 'making it' in English football continues unabated in the 21st century and, one imagines, will not diminish in the near future.

At the beginning of the 2013/14 English league season, there were 229 registered players – including reserve and youth team players – eligible to play for the Republic of

Ireland, who were attached to clubs in England's four professional leagues.

Of those 229 players, 153 were born in the Republic of Ireland; a further six (Shane Duffy, Paul George, Darron Gibson, James McClean, Eunan O'Kane and Marc Wilson) were born within the six counties of Northern Ireland; while two others (Noe Baba and Sean Maguire) were born in Cameroon and England respectively but were raised in Ireland and, subsequently, class themselves (and rightly so) as Irish.

And yet, at the same time, three English Premier League clubs (Chelsea, Southampton and Swansea City) had no Irish players in the 2013/14 season, including at youth/academy level, and there were no Irish players in the first-team squads at Manchester United, Manchester City, Chelsea, Arsenal and Tottenham Hotspur – the Premier League's top five at the conclusion of the 2012/13 season.

Everton, who finished sixth in 2012/13, included Seamus Coleman (Donegal) and Darron Gibson (Derry) in their squad, and have since signed Irish internationals James McCarthy and Aiden McGeady; both were born in Scotland before opting to represent Ireland.

Both McCarthy and McGeady are important players for Martin O'Neill, who was appointed senior team manager of the Republic of Ireland in 2013. In his playing career, O'Neill honed his midfield skills in his hometown, Derry, and played 64 times for Northern Ireland, including at the 1982 World Cup, where he captained the side to the quarter-finals.

He played almost 300 times for Nottingham Forest, between 1971 and 1981, when they were among the big-hitters in English football, winning the league title and two European Cups between 1977 and 1980.

And he told me, while pondering why Irish players no longer play for England's major clubs: 'When I went to England, in the early 1970s, it was a time when players from Ireland, both north and south, were not only playing for top English sides but instead were highly influential players for their clubs. You look at Pat Jennings, Sammy McIlroy, Sammy Nelson and Pat Rice from the north, and Liam Brady, David O'Leary and Frank Stapleton from the south – they were very important stars for their clubs. You look at Ronnie Whelan, for Liverpool, and he was a key figure in some significant moments in Liverpool's history. There were many influential Scottish players, too.'

Though the first non-British / Irish-born player to feature in England's top division was Tottenham's Max Seeburg in 1908, England's top flight was dominated by British and Irish players until the inception of the Premier League in 1992.

Historically, both Liverpool and Manchester United, the most trophy-laden institutions in English football, consistently boasted a healthy smattering of Irish players – even during the most triumphant moments in their histories.

For example, when Liverpool won the English First Division in 1980, their 12th league crown, they led a top four consisting of runners-up Manchester United, Ipswich Town and Arsenal. Between those teams there were seven Irish-born players, including four (Liam Brady, John Devine, David O'Leary and Frank Stapleton) at the top London side, Arsenal. Another two players (Ipswich's Kevin O'Callaghan and the then Liverpool and future

Everton player, Kevin Sheedy) were born in England but eligible to represent Ireland.

Ten years later, as Liverpool again won the league, five Irish-born players (Liverpool's Steve Staunton and Ronnie Whelan; Aston Villa's Paul McGrath; and Arsenal's David O'Leary and Niall Quinn) featured for teams to finish in the top four. Arsenal fringe player Kwame Ampadu was born in England but relocated to Ireland at a young age while Liverpool's John Aldridge and Ray Houghton, Aston Villa's Tony Cascarino and Tottenham's Chris Hughton were born in either England or Scotland and held the right to play for Ireland.

But fast forward to the end of the 2012/13 season and the Irish were only noticeable in top-four clubs by their complete absence.

By the 2009/2010 season, observers were seeing genuinely worrying signs about the significance of Irish players to leading English clubs. Chelsea won the Premier League with no Irish players in their first team, though Dubliner Conor Clifford was a regular for their reserves. Clifford has since dropped down the league ranks and returned to League of Ireland football in 2017.

Runners-up Manchester United, meanwhile, had two Irishmen (Darron Gibson and John O'Shea) but third-placed Arsenal had none, while Tottenham Hotspur, in fourth, had Robbie Keane as their sole representative from this part of the world.

If one delved further into the gut of these four clubs, in the 2009/10 season, the trend of looking elsewhere for young talent – other than Ireland – was highly evident from a varied list of nationalities represented in their squads.

For example, Arsenal's first-team squad contained players from Brazil, Cameroon, Ivory Coast, Mexico, Poland and Russia. The Tottenham squad, for the same season, boasted players from Honduras, Iceland, Mexico, Russia and Sweden. English clubs, it seemed, were reaching out – but turning a cold shoulder to the Emerald Isle.

By the 2013/14 season, the multinational make-up of English club squads was even more diverse. Chelsea's first-team squad included players from Australia, Egypt, Senegal and Serbia, while Arsenal had a Japanese player, Ryo Miyaichi. Manchester City and Liverpool had, among others, players from Argentina, Bosnia & Herzegovina, Ghana, Montenegro, Morocco, Nigeria and Uruguay. None of the aforementioned four clubs had any Irish players in their first-team squads and if one looked to the underbelly in each club – the reserve and youth teams – the relevance of Irish players appeared fairly insignificant with neither Chelsea nor Arsenal having one Irish-born player in the ranks.

In the Chelsea reserves, in 2013/14, were players from Burkina Faso, Chile, Colombia, Ghana, Nigeria and Uruguay, while Arsenal's reserves (for the same season) contained players from Argentina, Bolivia, Macedonia and Rwanda. Liverpool and Manchester City had three Irish players (combined), including the goalkeeper Ian Lawlor at the latter. Lawlor, however, has since dropped down the divisions to England's fourth tier.

But again, the tendency for English clubs – from senior level down to the academies – to look far and wide for young recruits was completely obvious by the fact that 20 countries, from four continents, were represented in the reserve teams of Liverpool and Manchester City (in 2013/14).

Make no mistake, the top English clubs cut no corners in finding the best young players in the world and they saturate the foreign market with their own coaching academies, usually run in the summer to teach children in other parts of the world how to play 'the Chelsea Way' or 'the Liverpool Way'.

They send coaching delegations to Malaysia, Philippines, Singapore and Thailand, where Chelsea host International Soccer Schools, or to China, India and South Africa, where Manchester United do likewise. Arsenal and Liverpool are also prominent in countries across Asia and Africa, with Arsenal holding regular Soccer Schools in a host of US locations from Connecticut to Florida and New York to Washington.

In an interview with Tony Leen for the *Irish Examiner*, having just announced his retirement from his academy role at Arsenal, the former Ireland midfielder Liam Brady says: 'We [Arsenal] probably have around 20 scouts on the payroll around the world and they're very good. The likes of Gilles Grimandi in France would have pushed for Sagna, Koscielny, Sanogo, Giroud. You scout every corner of the globe. You have to. Because if there's a great 16-year-old in Argentina, you can bet your life Manchester City will also know about him.'

The level of difficulty in emerging from the raft of youth and reserve team players to become a first-team player is difficult to quantify, as are the exact numbers of Irish players going to England each year, either for trials or to sign permanently, as the Football Association of Ireland doesn't have an organised database for recording the information. But according to Eoin Hand, a former Ireland player and manager, anywhere between 20 and 25 Irish players sign with English clubs every year. Hand is certainly in the know. A former player with Portsmouth and manager of Huddersfield Town, he was employed by the FAI from 1999 to 2012, initially as a career guidance officer with a mandate to help young players going to or coming back from English clubs.

His role was expanded in 2004 with the former Drumcondra star taking on the role of football support services manager, which included advising Irish clubs in negotiations with overseas clubs looking to sign young Irish players.

Eoin told me that the instances of Irish players moving to England increased dramatically in the wake of the success of Brian Kerr's underage international sides in the late 1990s, when Irish teams won the UEFA Under-16 and Under-18 European Championships and finished third at the 1997 World Youth Championships.

'You had about 20 players, more or less, going annually before then. But when English clubs noticed Brian Kerr's teams, the figure rose to between 30 and 35 per year, for an eight-to-ten-year period from the late 1990s. The figure has levelled off again in recent years to between 20 and 25 per year. Sure, it's become more difficult to make it with the really top clubs but I would say that, contrary to media sensationalism, about 80 per cent of our players manage to progress to make a good career in the English game. It's not always with the club they signed for initially. In fact, it rarely is. But the figure of players remaining in English football, where they enjoy lengthy and fruitful careers, is greater than people imagine,' says Hand.

'However,' he adds, 'it has become far more difficult for young players to make the grade at the top clubs. They are recruiting from a worldwide base and buying ready-made stars.

'We don't see many cases like Gerry Daly, John Giles, Ashley Grimes, Frank Stapleton, Liam Brady, Ronnie Whelan and many more – all lads that went to top English clubs and made a big impact.'

Notwithstanding the fact that at least 20 Irish players join English clubs each year, the demise of Irish players has been such that by 2013, Ireland had fallen from the second most prolific supplier of players to England's top flight to the fourth. Scotland, once leading the way, had slumped to seventh.

Due to the decreasing chances of Irish players breaking into the first teams in England's top flight, the natural result is that more and more Irish players are dropping into the lower divisions and, in some cases, transferring to Scottish clubs, where the standard of the top division is undoubtedly less skilled than in England's glamorous Premier League.

Again, the statistics make for depressing reading. On the opening day of the 2013/14 English Football League season (for the second, third and fourth tiers), 39 Irish-born players started matches for teams in the English Championship, League 1 and League 2, while only ten Irish-born players took to the field on the opening day of the 2013/14 Premier League season.

Fourteen Irish-born players made ten or more appearances for Premier League teams in the 2013/14 season with a further eight Irish-qualified players (born outside Ireland) also doing so.

But none of those 22 players (including those born outside Ireland) played for teams that finished in the top four, while only five featured for teams that finished the season in the top half of the Premier League. Furthermore, only six Irish-born players played 30 or more games for Premier League clubs in the 2013/14 season, with an additional three Irish-qualified players (born outside Ireland) reaching that mark.

The figures for the English Championship (second tier) were very different with 25 Irish-born players and a further 16 Irish-qualified players making ten or more first-team appearances in the 2013/14 season. Seventeen of the 25 Irish-born players reached the 30-plus threshold for the season while nine Irish-qualified players (born outside Ireland) did likewise.

Martin O'Neill and the FAI have no reason not to be cognisant of the diminishing importance of Irish players. O'Neill, for example, could only name three players born on the island and under the age of 25 (Robbie Brady, Seamus Coleman and James McClean) when selecting his first Irish squad, in November 2013, while as if to illustrate a paucity of new talent coming into the senior side, Ireland (at that time) were still reliant on the country's all-time leading goalscorer, Robbie Keane (then 34 and playing in the United States) for the majority of their goals. However, when I got the opportunity to speak briefly with the FAI chief executive officer, John Delaney in July 2014, he appeared less perturbed by the shortage of Irish players turning out for England's top sides.

'I think it's a concern for England, Scotland, Ireland and Wales. The English Premier League, as we all know, is dominated by foreign players, coaches and club owners, and that's in line with the overall globalisation of the game. We're talking around 70 per cent of Premier League players not coming from the traditional source, the so-called Home Nations, but within all that, Ireland has some very good players operating at an elite level in England,' he says.

He pointed to Ireland's quartet of Everton players, including James McCarthy and Aiden McGeady, whose football educations had been spent in their country of birth, Scotland.

However, Seamus Coleman's selection for the 2013/14 Professional Footballers' Association (PFA) Team of the Year was the first time an Irish player had made the exclusive selection since Richard Dunne – as an Aston Villa player – in 2009/10. Other than Coleman and Dunne, only six Irish players have made the Team of the Year since the turn of the century.

Irish players are also making minimal impact on the scoresheet in the Premier League, with Everton right-back Coleman and Shane Long (then of Hull City) top-scoring with seven goals in the 2013/14 season. Stoke City's Jon Walters (born in England) was the only other Irish-qualified player to score five goals in the season.

Martin O'Neill said he remains hopeful that the Irish will re-emerge in England's top league, but all the while more and more Irish players attached to Premier League clubs are being 'loaned' to lower league clubs, usually on the premise of gaining much-needed first-team experience. Unlike in some continental countries, most specifically in Italy where the loan market has been rampant for some time, the use of the loan system by English clubs only took off around the summer of 2007.

Between ten transfer windows from the summer of 2009 to January 2014, 136 Irish-born players were involved in loan moves between clubs in England (some more than once). Generally, the movement involved Premier League or Championship players transferring, for a set period of time, to clubs in the lower leagues.

To illustrate the relatively new-found buoyancy of England's loan market, the previous ten transfer windows (summer 2004 to January 2009) saw just 41 Irish-born players involved in loan moves.

Sometimes young players are 'loaned' with the intention of gaining worthwhile experience in a competitive environment. That's one way for young players to view such moves and is something with which to console themselves at an uncertain juncture in their careers.

In reality though, the vast majority of players loaned from clubs in England's top two divisions to lower league clubs rarely return to long-term careers with their parent clubs. More likely, a loan move to a lower league club is the first step in preparing players for their eventual release or permanent transfer from the parent club. Such transfers inevitably see the previously 'loaned' player sign permanently for a lower league club, thus joining a stockpile of Irish players deemed surplus to requirements at the top and only good enough for a lesser standard.

The impact this has on Irish players is most noticeable at international level when players of limited quality are asked to perform against world-class talent on the international stage.

In many such cases, it is simply asking too much of the players to raise their game sufficiently and hold their own against opposing players that compete, week in, week out, in some of Europe's top divisions.

For example, how can Ireland expect second tier players to one week compete against journeymen Championship midfielders and then against the cream of Europe's midfield talent like Andrés Iniesta (Barcelona), Luka Modrić (Real Madrid) and Andrea Pirlo (Juventus), all of whom excelled against a limited Irish team at the 2014 European Championships? Yes, the Irish players will never be short on perspiration, pride and desire. But it is plainly asking too much of them to compete with the very best at international level.

Before recently rejoining the top 30 in the official FIFA rankings, the Irish team had slid alarmingly from a peak position of sixth, in 1993, to its lowest ever placing (70th) in July 2014.

When Ireland qualified for the country's first ever appearance at a major international finals, the 1988 European Championships, the squad boasted three players from Liverpool, two from Manchester United and one from Arsenal. There was one player each from Everton, Newcastle United and Tottenham Hotspur, while three players were attached to Celtic in Scotland. The squad contained just two players from England's second tier: David Kelly (Walsall) and Gerry Peyton (Bournemouth).

Two years later, when Jack Charlton's Ireland qualified for the 1990 World Cup, the squad still contained three Liverpool players. Two came from Aston Villa while Arsenal, Everton and Tottenham Hotspur supplied a player apiece. Celtic were again represented by two players.

By the time Ireland competed at the 1994 World Cup in the United States, the squad included four players operating in England's second tier; however, it still contained players from some of England's most renowned clubs including two from Manchester United and Manchester City, three from Aston Villa, and one apiece from Arsenal, Chelsea, Leeds United and Liverpool. Two players were also performing in Scotland's top flight.

By 2002, though, when Ireland travelled to the World Cup in Japan and South Korea, Manchester United were still represented in the squad (by Roy Keane) but his premature departure left the squad with no players from the top four clubs in the Premier League (Manchester United, Arsenal, Liverpool and Newcastle United).

Instead, six clubs that finished tenth or lower in the 2001/02 Premier League season were represented in the squad. And when Ireland next appeared at a major tournament in 2012, six of the squad were registered to English second tier clubs.

Damningly, Aaron Callaghan, who played for Stoke City in the 1980s and is now a respected coach in Ireland, says that the fortunes of Irish players, and those of the national team, are unlikely to change.

'It's not going to change for Irish players. It's difficult enough to get young English players into Premier League teams – never mind young Irish ones. And it's hard to imagine the situation changing in the near future,' he says.

Whatever major events occur in English football in the next few years, they are likely to happen without the input of Irish players, who are not yet a dying breed in English football but are, most definitely, an ever-dwindling force.

A source for hope is the emergence of a clear desire from the English FA to implement change to the way

Premier League clubs produce and give opportunities to home-grown players. Of course, any changes would be motivated mainly by a desire to secure a better future for the England team. Yet, if some of the proposals put forward by the now departed chairman Mr Dyke, which are too plentiful to examine in full here, are eventually ushered in, they could, almost by accident, aid the cause of Irish players.

Before then, however, Ireland and the FAI need to help themselves. Later, I will look at proposals to change the way that Irish children are taught to play the game. First, though, it is imperative to remind ourselves of the players from Ireland's rich football past, who once propelled the country to the front of people's minds when considering football, as these players can teach us valuable lessons about what it takes to reach – and to remain – at the very top level in the game.

Chapter 2

The Way We Were

I F YOU turn to page 18 of Paddy Agnew's splendid
book *Forza Italia: A Journey in Search of Italy and
Its Football*, there is a wonderful, almost emotional
passage about one of the greatest Irishmen to play the
game of football, Liam Brady.

With Agnew fresh to Italian life, having been assigned
the role of covering the Italian game, his eyes were firmly
fixed on securing an interview with the Dublin star, who
had signed for Italian giants Juventus after a wonderful
seven seasons in the heart of the Arsenal midfield.

And here is what Agnew, remembering those halcyon
days for Brady, and for Irish footballers making a mark on
foreign soil, had to say: 'In those days, Brady was a Serie A
icon. All you had to say was that you were Irish and Italians
would often reply, "Ah, like Liam Brady." When Italian
football re-opened its frontiers to foreign stars in the
1980s, Brady was the first foreigner purchased by Italy's
most famous club, Juventus. In seven seasons between

1973 and 1980 at Arsenal, he had established himself as one of the brightest talents in European football. In two title-winning seasons with Juventus, and subsequently in two years with newly promoted Sampdoria, Brady played probably the best football of his tremendous career. His close control, vision, passing and silken left foot were always destined to shine brightly in the Serie A of the 1980s – a cerebral, tactical league that was light years from the hurly-burly of the (then) English First Division. Brady played great football, spoke good Italian, and was widely admired and respected.'

Back then, Irish players had it all. Like Brady, there were countless others to shine at the top of their profession. And while Brady's career took him beyond England's shores and the rough and tumble of its late 1970s and 1980s football, to a more cultured existence in the then most competitive league in the world, the rest of Ireland's leading lights from the period would largely remain in the confines of English football.

Not that remaining there, however, would affect their impact in overall European club competitions with the likes of Denis Irwin, Roy Keane and Ronnie Whelan all getting their hands on the continent's greatest club football prize, the European Cup (UEFA Champions League when Irwin and Keane won with Manchester United in 1999), while before then, John Giles had spearheaded Leeds United's two UEFA Cup successes in the 1970s.

And that's before we even consider the impact of the Irish in domestic English football, where between them the aforementioned Irwin and Keane (Manchester United) and Whelan (Liverpool) won an astounding 20 top-flight league titles combined. All the while, others like Paul McGrath and Kevin Moran would win the prestigious FA Cup with Manchester United, and David O'Leary and Niall Quinn would help Arsenal win the league title in 1987; a feat repeated by O'Leary in 1991. The Irish were everywhere. And they were integral to their respective club sides.

They were not merely satisfied with just joining English clubs. They were signing for the very best; the clubs who had expectations of winning trophies annually. Their skill and undying will to win was welcomed with open arms by England's major football institutions and instead of feeling inferior to English colleagues, they would rise to the challenge and add outrageous quality to the ranks. The Irish were prized assets.

Yet times have changed, dramatically. And now, thanks to the enormous pressure placed on the top clubs to keep winning, and their financial ability to sign any player from around the world, the sight of a fresh-faced Irish teenager making his debut for one of England's major sides – those regularly vying to qualify for the UEFA Champions League through a top-four league finish – is disappointingly rare.

The worldwide transfer market has opened up beyond recognition, meaning it has become far more commonplace to see young South Americans, Africans or players from mainland Europe, like France and Germany, making Premier League bows ahead of players from the United Kingdom and Ireland.

Indeed, while Manchester City, the Premier League champions from 2012 and 2014 and a genuine financial powerhouse in modern football, were blooding the exciting Brazilian teenager Gabriel Jesus in the second half of the 2016/17 season, Dublin-born midfielder Jack Byrne, once tipped by Irish football observers as one who might come through for City, was searching to find his way in his career. First, he spent time on loan with the Dutch side Cambuur before a similar temporary move to English Championship side Blackburn Rovers saw 20-year-old Byrne struggle for game-time and eventually leave on a permanent transfer to Championship strugglers Wigan Athletic.

The contrast in fortunes for Jesus and Byrne is stark, indeed. For while Jesus now seems destined to become one of world football's brightest young stars, Byrne, in some ways, is going back to the start, looking to prove his worth again at a lower level. But Byrne's situation is not an isolated one, for only a few weeks before he was moved on by mega-rich City, goalkeeper Ian Lawlor, a fellow Irishman, had also severed his ties with the club to find more regular football, moving to England's fourth tier with Doncaster Rovers.

Both players have become recent victims of the global nature of the modern English game. And while it is somewhat hypothetical, one cannot help but wonder how they would have developed had they been born in a different era, particularly when you consider that Byrne was once compared by Patrick Vieira (then Man City's youth team coach) to Manchester United's legendary midfielder Paul Scholes.

Instead, the bulk of those selected to join English sides are now travelling in hope rather than in expectation, as the reality of just how difficult it is to make a mark in the modern era has become so patently obvious. It seems like the challenges that they meet, in England, are greater than ever before.

And yet, the Ireland senior team manager Martin O'Neill wonders if the country's hopeful young players are doing enough after arriving in English football.

'In general, some young boys in the Premier League get handed things far too easy. And they quickly form the opinion that this way of being treated is the norm. It certainly can take away a bit of the hunger and desire to continue improving and to make a long-term impression at their club and in their career,' he says.

'However,' he adds, 'I wonder if young Irish boys should use the huge level of competition as an excuse for not achieving lengthy careers? When Liam Brady went to Arsenal, for example, do you think he thought, "Well, we'll see how it goes but the odds are against me making it here?" No, he was determined not only to go to England and join a top side like Arsenal, but to become a really top player in the English game. The same way of thinking applied to a lot of Irish players that went to England in the 1970s and 1980s. I am not saying that young players are less determined nowadays but what I am saying is that you have to have a certain spirit, within yourself, to get over there and to defy the odds, regardless of the level of competition.'

That spirit and defiance that O'Neill refers to was probably last seen, from an Irish perspective, in defensive lynchpin Richard Dunne, who unlike Byrne and Lawlor was able to crack the City first team having joined from Everton in 2000. He would make over 300 appearances for City, where his contribution is still respected by City fans. And in some ways, perhaps Dunne's determination to succeed as a professional, having been discarded by his first English club (Everton), can serve as a beacon of hope and inspiration to young Irish players in England, like Byrne and Lawlor, who could still yet come back stronger.

But Dunne himself says that the mentality of young players in the English game has changed beyond recognition in recent decades.

'Look, I see it all the time,' Dunne says. 'Young kids, who have done nothing in the game, with the flash car, designer clothes, the gold watches. It's not great to see – but you can barely avoid it.'

'That side of the game never appealed to me,' he continues. 'I was on £45 a week after joining Everton and couldn't afford a flight home. It's just not like that any more. Everything has changed and the young players have far more power and money than before. Young players need to realise that you don't go from nowhere to the very top and that the ones fortunate enough to reach the top have worked hard to get there.

'I don't think the majority of young players grasp that. I remember being told [at Everton] that I would not be there for ever but that it was up to me to dictate the manner that I would eventually leave – whether out of the front door having worked hard and learned enough to continue as a professional or through the back door, offloaded because I hadn't applied myself or grasped the opportunity.

'Some young players reckon they can stroll into another team if they are released by a big Premier League club. But it doesn't happen like that and you have to put the shoulder to the wheel and make a lot of sacrifices to enjoy a lengthy career in the Premier League. The money in the game is a bit ridiculous but it's the ones who stay out of the limelight in their teens that deservedly reap the sporting and financial rewards,' adds Dunne, who was part of a golden generation of Irish players like Damien Duff (who won two Premier League titles with Chelsea), Shay Given (who won the FA Cup with Manchester City) and Robbie Keane (Ireland's leading goalscorer in international football), who managed to defy the odds to progress to the Ireland side and prolonged success in the Premier League.

That quartet were wonderful servants to their country, and the only star names in an otherwise distinctly average Irish side that foundered hopelessly at the 2012 European Championships, a tournament that provided a sour end to the international careers of Duff and Dunne, who along with Given and Robbie Keane were always the players whom Ireland fans looked to for leadership and quality once the magnificent Roy Keane retired from international football in 2005.

Between them, Given, Duff and Keane had the ability to alter the outcome of games in Ireland's favour and for a period they were labelled as truly world class.

But what made Dunne so special, you ask?

After all, was he not the archetypal Irish centre-half? Was he anything but another physically imposing defender with nothing but brute strength and bravery?

No. For club and country, for 20 years, Dunne had a remarkable gift for inspiring those around him in a career that spanned over 400 Premier League games and 13 years in the Irish senior team; the apogee of which came in Moscow when he produced an almost superhuman effort in the 2012 European Championships qualifier against Russia.

Previously, Ireland had never got any sort of result in the Russian capital but they desperately needed a draw (at least) to stay on track for a play-off berth in the 2012 qualifiers. Russia had been the best team in the qualifying group and were already assured of finishing top of the group. They had also dismissed Ireland with relative ease early in the group, in Dublin.

What unfolded on a typically freezing night at the Luzhniki Stadium – and particularly in the second half – was a varied and potentially lethal cocktail of dangerous Russian attacks. The Irish side looked certain to wilt at various points, as the Russians seemed to just keep coming at the goal.

It was truly one of those games, as an Irish supporter, where you tended to watch through fingers covering your eyes. You felt like a Russian goal would come. It seemed like a matter of time.

Yet, thanks to the inspirational Dunne, who produced two unbelievable blocks to prevent certain goals, the game would end scoreless. Dunne finished the match with four stitches to a head wound and his display earned rave reviews, in particular from the great Paul McGrath, who described the performance as the best he ever saw from an Irish centre-half.

The display would earn Dunne the nickname of 'The Iron Curtain', while one popular Irish sports website wrote to government minister Alan Shatter to request that 6 September (the date of the match) be officially declared as 'Richard Dunne Day'.

Meanwhile, the *College Tribune*, a student newspaper in University College Dublin, carried 'A Testimonial to Richard Dunne', in which writer Eoghan Glynn described

Dunne as 'a man we can trust, who would leave himself bloodied and battered for the sake of his country'.

In the eyes of many, Dunne's amazing show of strength in Moscow helped cement his place on a lengthy list of truly great Irish players – those to shine for their country while also gracing England's top flight with consistent distinction – going back to the 1940s when Johnny Carey captained Manchester United for seven seasons.

The legendary Carey, from County Dublin, was one of the first Irishmen to become a long-term fixture at one of England's greatest clubs, and the versatile defender would make in excess of 400 appearances (in two spells) for the Old Trafford side. Usually a full-back, Carey was the first non-UK player and the first Irishman to captain winning sides in both the English First Division and the FA Cup. Before signing for United for £250, Carey had played for two months in the League of Ireland for St James's Gate before catching the eye of United talent-spotter Billy Behan, who engineered a move.

Carey would never look back and he won the Football Writers' Association Footballer of the Year Award in 1949, and played in the Irish side that famously beat England at Goodison Park in the same year. While still an active player, Carey took charge of the Ireland team for the 1948 Olympic Games and in 1953, shortly after retiring, he became the manager of Blackburn Rovers.

Carey's wonderful impact at Old Trafford would pave the way for a succession of top-class Irish players to play for United including the equally outstanding Noel Cantwell, Tony Dunne, John Giles, Paul McGrath, Kevin Moran and, more recently, the Cork duo of Denis Irwin and Roy Keane.

Also born in Dublin, Tony Dunne was another Old Trafford hero, playing 530 games for United after moving from Shelbourne in 1960, only a week after helping Shelbourne win the FAI Cup.

A former Stella Maris schoolboy, the 33-times capped international would win two league titles with United, as well as the 1963 FA Cup, and was part of the United side that won the 1968 European Cup, beating Benfica of Portugal in the final. To this day, Dunne remains seventh in the list of Manchester United's record all-time appearance makers behind fellow club legends Ryan Giggs, Bobby Charlton, Bill Foulkes, Paul Scholes, Gary Neville and Alex Stepney.

For seven years, Dunne was joined in the United side by County Cork's Noel Cantwell, who had captained West Ham United to the English Second Division title before transferring to Old Trafford. Cantwell would win two league titles for United and captained the side that won the 1963 FA Cup Final.

Dunne, who was also a respected cricketer, and fellow Dubliner John Giles, would also feature for United in the 1963 FA Cup Final before Cantwell retired in 1967 having claimed 36 international caps. He then managed Coventry City and Peterborough United, as well as serving as the chairman of the English Professional Footballers' Association.

And the Irish links to Old Trafford would carry through to the early stages of the Premier League, as Denis Irwin and Roy Keane became club legends by winning multiple major honours. They were joined in the side by utility player John O'Shea, who never quite got the credit he deserved for winning five league titles with United before moving to Sunderland, while Darron Gibson, an Irish international born in County Derry, would be a more peripheral figure for United in a seven-year spell that included a league title in 2011 but just over 30 league appearances in total.

The departure from Old Trafford of Gibson (to Everton) and O'Shea arguably ended the Irish association with England's major clubs. But in the 1970s and 1980s, Ireland could boast a number of supremely talented players competing at the highest echelon in the English game.

For while John Giles had left Old Trafford to inspire Leeds United to the title in 1974 (his second at Elland Road), the midfield genius Liam Brady was fast becoming the darling of the Arsenal supporters having debuted in 1973. And despite the league title evading Brady in seven wonderful years in north London, he is still worshipped among supporters of the Gunners.

Stuart Stratford, who runs the Arsenal online blog 'A Cultured Left Foot' and contributed to a brilliant Arsenal anthology called *So Paddy Got Up*, said that Brady played a significant role in Arsenal's proud history.

'Brady became a pivotal member of the team and the fulcrum around which the squad was built,' Stratford recalls.

'Arsenal supporters loved young players who came through the ranks. Okay, Brady didn't come off the North Bank, like Charlie George did, but he was as close to "one of us" as can be imagined.'

Despite not winning the league (the highest position Arsenal finished with Brady was fourth), Brady was integral to the Gunners reaching three FA Cup Finals.

Arsenal were surprisingly beaten in the 1978 and 1980 finals by Ipswich Town and West Ham United, but Brady would play a significant role in all three Arsenal goals as they defeated Manchester United in the 1979 decider.

That day, he was joined in the Arsenal side by fellow Irishmen David O'Leary and Frank Stapleton, the latter scoring in the final before transferring to Old Trafford.

Brady, O'Leary and Stapleton are significant players in Arsenal's past, although it would kill many Arsenal supporters to acknowledge Stapleton's legacy because of his transfer to United. O'Leary, for example, would play for Arsenal for 19 years, making 772 appearances and winning league titles in 1989 and 1991.

In stark contrast to the limited chances afforded to young Irish players these days, O'Leary had stepped into the Arsenal side at 17. And Dave Faber, who writes brilliantly on www.goonerholic.com, remembers O'Leary breaking into the Gunners' side.

'Barely looking his age, David looked all arms and legs and was quickly nicknamed "Spider",' he recalls.

'But never judge a book by its cover,' he continues.

'The fans loved O'Leary from the start and he gave astonishing service to Arsenal. Only Tony Adams would be mentioned with more affection.'

O'Leary spent almost two years captaining Arsenal and also won two FA Cups and two League Cups before joining Leeds United, where he would later manage, on a free transfer in 1993.

'O'Leary was quite simply a rare breed,' Faber adds.

'Even at 17, he was a player comfortable with the ball at his feet and happy to carry it forward to look for an intelligent pass in an era when lumping the ball forward was fashionable. Few players got the better of him in the air and those who thought him vulnerable to pace were surprised. Nothing flustered him. Softly spoken he may have been, but he was a leader under successive managers who favoured strong characters.'

Despite winning 68 Irish caps, O'Leary's international career would be encapsulated in two major incidents. The first happened in the early stages of Jack Charlton's tenure. Having made his debut in 1976, O'Leary was surprisingly omitted from Charlton's squad for a mini-tournament in Iceland in 1986. When several of the chosen players withdrew, O'Leary was summoned for duty, but having booked a family holiday after the squad was initially announced, he decided that family came first and refused to cancel the holiday. As a result, O'Leary would not feature for Ireland in over two years, thus missing the country's 1988 European Championships adventure.

The second incident is more cheery and hopefully how most Irish fans best remember O'Leary. At the 1990 World Cup, the country's debut appearance in the tournament, Ireland played against Romania in the last 16 stage. The match would end scoreless after extra time and went to a penalty shoot-out. When Packie Bonner saved from Daniel Timofte's penalty (Romania's fifth), O'Leary had the task of putting Ireland into the quarter-finals.

A substitute in the match, O'Leary calmly fired the ball past the Romanian goalkeeper and into the net, sending a nation into a state of widespread celebration, and the team into the last eight, ensuring that his penalty will always be recalled as one of the outstanding moments in Irish sporting history.

On each occasion that O'Leary helped Arsenal to win the league, their closest challengers had been Liverpool, who consistently showed strong allegiances to Irish players in the 1980s with the likes of Jim Beglin, Steve Staunton and Ronnie Whelan. Liverpool also fielded Ireland internationals John Aldridge, Mark Lawrenson and Ray Houghton (all born outside Ireland), who made a major mark with the Merseyside club, while the Dublin-born Steve Heighway, who was brought up in England, was a majestic player for Liverpool between 1970 and 1981, winning four league titles and a couple of European Cups.

Like Heighway, Ronnie Whelan was involved in many of Liverpool's greatest nights, winning six league titles and the European Cup in 15 years at Anfield. Indeed, when a poll was taken of 110,000 Liverpool supporters to establish the '100 Players Who Shook The Kop', Whelan came in 30th.

Whelan also made an impression in international football, making 53 appearances for his country, and his spectacular volleyed goal against the Soviet Union, as Ireland almost emerged from a tough group that included England and Holland at the 1988 European Championships, was the stuff of dreams (though many still try to take the good out of it by stressing that Whelan's effort came off his shin!).

On that occasion, in fact, Ireland probably played the best passing football ever managed under Jack Charlton's stewardship. Charlton had preferred a well-thought-out but quite direct style of play, which reaped massive rewards for an Irish team who had previously failed to reach any major tournament. His disciplined game plan hurried opponents into mistakes and minimised the chance of the

Irish team making costly errors in possession, and it took the Irish team to its first ever competitive tournament in 1988. There, they managed a euphoric victory against neighbours England in the opening group match, thanks to a solitary Ray Houghton goal, a fair portion of good fortune and good goalkeeping by Packie Bonner. But it was against the Soviet Union, a team packed with outstanding technical players, when Ireland really stood up on the international stage, to show people what Irish players were truly capable of.

Seeing that the Soviets were hesitant to close them down, the Irish players grasped the nettle themselves, showing initiative and enough poise and technical expertise to be able to outplay the eastern Europeans at their own game. For many Irish supporters, the performance, though ultimately garnering just a 1-1 draw, was the real moment that the Irish arrived on the big stage. For instead of relying on their opponents to fluff their lines and play into the hands of Charlton's crafty approach, they dictated the tempo and flow of the game themselves against a Soviet side who went on to lose in the final.

Within six years the Irish team had qualified for two World Cups, where the genuine quality of some of the players really shone brightly; perhaps none more so than in the mesmeric defensive performances of Paul McGrath, whose career in England started at Manchester United, where he was an FA Cup winner in the mid-1980s.

McGrath played in over 150 games for United but had joined Aston Villa by the time he played in his first World Cup, in 1990. Perhaps McGrath would have played longer for United had he not been part of an apparently raging drinking culture in the club before the arrival, as manager, of Alex Ferguson.

After he was named man of the match in the 1985 FA Cup Final, for holding United together after a red card for fellow Irish defender Kevin Moran (the first ever red card in the FA Cup Final), it seemed like McGrath was destined for long-term greatness in United colours. Yet Ferguson had different ideas and with injuries playing an enormous role in his career, McGrath was sold on to Aston Villa.

Despite his personal demons and woefully suspect knees, which completely curtailed how much training he could do, McGrath's natural ability would always see him through and even though he might have stayed at Old Trafford longer, he did go on to become a legend at Aston Villa, who very nearly won the league in McGrath's debut season.

With McGrath in imperious form, as usual, Villa would finish second in the league, behind Liverpool, and McGrath then went on to play a crucial role in the Villans' League Cup wins of 1994 and 1996. Affectionately known to the Villa fans as 'God', McGrath could do everything a defender needed to do. And despite a fairly languid running style, he was deceptively quick and gifted at reading the play.

Indeed, Dave Woodhall of the 'Heroes & Villains' website was left gobsmacked by McGrath's class – even after just one pre-season game against Hibernian from Scotland.

'Ball comes over, McGrath is waiting, knowing full well where it is going to be, and in one movement kills it. And without looking he delivers a first-time pass into the path of a Villa player. And so a legend was born in that simple but so effective execution. That season, his first, was a great one, as Villa finished unexpected league runners-up. The team exceeded expectation and McGrath stood head and shoulders above the rest,' he remembers.

'The supreme McGrath moment though, came in a match against QPR at Villa Park,' he continues.

'Their forward was through one-on-one with goalkeeper Nigel Spink. There was no way McGrath could get a tackle in without giving away a penalty. Except that he did. And not only did he stop the attack but he came out with the ball and laid it off for a Villa player. McGrath clenched his fist and you could see him muttering "yesss", knowing the bit of magic he had brought off. As one, the crowd – both the Villa and Rangers supporters – rose to acclaim something special.'

McGrath would eventually leave Aston Villa in 1996 to play for Derby County and then Sheffield United before retiring in 1998, aged 38. He also played for Ireland on 83 occasions and although Jack Charlton often used him in midfield, it was in defence where McGrath displayed true prowess and game intelligence, especially in the opening match of the 1994 World Cup against Italy. For as much as Ray Houghton's goal helped the Irish to an unlikely win, a victory would not have been possible without McGrath's defensive interventions, which helped prevent Roberto Baggio, Italy's gifted pony-tailed forward, from equalising.

Also playing for Ireland on the day was an all-action midfielder from Cork. Roy Keane had just helped Manchester United to a second successive league title, in his debut campaign at Old Trafford after moving from

Nottingham Forest, where his lengthy career had begun in style.

Keane was only 19 when first appearing in the top flight with Forest. And under the guidance of the legendary Brian Clough, his combative style would immediately win the hearts of the City Ground faithful, as the seeds were sown for the emergence of one of the game's great midfield players.

'The early impression [of Keane] was of a confident young player with very little, if any respect for opponents. He was in no way overawed and fitted into the top division like he had been playing there for years. Even then, Keane could really influence games,' recalls Kevin Reidy of the Nottingham Forest Irish Supporters' Club.

Keane would twice reach Wembley Stadium as a Forest player. But on both occasions – the 1991 FA Cup Final and 1992 League Cup Final – the combative midfielder would end up on the losing side.

Despite winning the Forest Player of the Year award at the end of the 1992/93 season, Keane's inspired performances could not prevent Forest's relegation from the Premier League. Nonetheless, his individual efforts had caught the attention of the Premier League big-boys with Manchester United eventually beating off competition from Blackburn Rovers for his signature, for a then British record fee of £3.75m.

Alex Ferguson had reinvigorated the fortunes of Manchester United since joining from Scottish club Aberdeen and saw Keane as the natural successor to veteran midfield warrior Bryan Robson. And in his debut season at Old Trafford the Corkman would win the Premier League and FA Cup double.

Having then become the United captain after the unexpected retirement of Eric Cantona in 1997, Keane recorded six more league titles, as United became the dominant force in England.

He won four more FA Cups and the UEFA Champions League, though he would not play in the final of the latter competition because of suspension.

That Keane missed United's memorable Champions League Final defeat of Bayern Munich in Barcelona in 1999 was one of the great tragedies of an illustrious career, particularly as Keane had been simply awesome in United's semi-final second leg comeback against Juventus; scoring the team's first goal as they fought from two goals down to win. Keane, however, received a yellow card for tripping Zinedine Zidane, which subsequently ruled him out of the final.

Yet, that unfortunate blot on Keane's sparkling career could never diminish his catalogue of achievements. And Chudi Onwuazor, co-editor of the United blog 'Pride Of All Europe", maintains that Keane was United's greatest player in the Alex Ferguson era.

'He had an unparalleled will to win that complemented his ability in the middle of the park. He was the club's most successful captain and a player the club has yet to replace,' he says.

After playing over 300 times for United, Keane unexpectedly left the club by mutual consent in 2005, leaving behind a legacy, as a captain and midfield enforcer, that seems unlikely to be matched in the future – and certainly not by a fellow Irish player.

Keane would then sign for Celtic, where he won the Scottish League and League Cup before taking over as manager of Sunderland, whom he steered to the English Championship title.

In 2006, Keane was afforded an emotional testimonial by United and almost 70,000 spectators showed up to pay tribute to an outstanding playing career.

Sadly, many people still believe that Keane's contribution to the Irish national team was irreparably damaged by the infamous Saipan incident when a torrid clash with Irish manager Mick McCarthy, just before the 2002 World Cup, led to Keane departing the squad training base and playing no part in the tournament.

Now, page upon page has been written about the controversial incident, from which, quite frankly, neither Keane nor McCarthy emerged with great credit. Ultimately, Keane's non-participation at the World Cup deprived the team of their on-field leader, which was a desperately sad loss ahead of Ireland's first World Cup appearance since 1994.

Without him leading the troops on the greatest international stage of all, Ireland still came within a whisker of the quarter-finals, only losing to Spain in a last 16 penalty shoot-out. And who knows what might have been achieved had the great Keane been there? After all, a fairly limited yet mightily organised (and quite fortunate) South Korean team would reach the semi-finals!

It is not my intention, however, to re-open the old gaping wounds from Saipan. For you could sit and argue for hours, maybe even for days, about the rights and wrongs from that regrettable moment in Irish football history. And when you allow yourself to do that, in some ways you get distracted from what really matters, to true football fans, about Roy Keane. And that, for me, was the inspirational, heroic fashion in which he played the game for both Ireland and his clubs.

Instead, I feel it's more important and cathartic to concentrate on what Keane, the player, brought to the Ireland set-up, having once been nothing more than an enthusiastic young player rejected by many English clubs, who as a teenager he would write to looking for trials.

Leaving aside Saipan, which some supporters still find difficult to do, his performances in the green shirt were most outstanding. You just felt safer with Keane in the team. And Manchester United fans would tell you the same. You knew that matters would never fall apart with Keane cajoling and controlling in the heart of midfield, harrying and hassling the opponent and doing so with enormous tactical acumen and understanding of the true role of an all-round central midfielder.

He just knew where to be, how to get there with minimum fuss and, more often than not, exactly what to do when he got there.

He had a desire and will to win that oozed powerfully from every pore, thus inspiring those who played with him and often putting the fear of God into his rivals.

Crucially, he was rarely inaccurate in his passing. Generally, they would be relatively short, sharp passes with the onus, as it should be, on treating the ball with care. That doesn't have to mean being conservative in possession, passing safely backwards or to the side. Keane was unopposed to doing so when the time was right, but his instinctive inclination would always be to at least try to move it forward. Having great players around him at United obviously aided such attempts.

Yet, the United side that won so many major honours in the 1990s would not have been the same without Keane. He was the driving force and leader. The Irish team, too, would always miss Keane greatly in his absence, despite some players, particularly in the 2002 World Cup, visibly doubling their contribution to plug the inevitable gaps caused by his loss.

So, instead of lamenting what might have happened in Saipan, this writer prefers to remember some of Keane's finest moments for his country. And most specifically his unreal contribution in the qualifying process for the 2002 World Cup, as Keane inspired Ireland, undefeated, through a tough group including big-hitting Holland and Portugal.

Keane's display in the home fixture against the former, for example, when Jason McAteer's goal ensured a famous victory, was absolutely scintillating. I was in the Lansdowne Road stands that day and have never since witnessed a more influential midfield display. I doubt that I ever will. Keane had the presence of two or three players on that occasion, getting stuck into the technically gifted Dutch players from the off and genuinely inspiring his team-mates. He could make the crowd believe that anything was possible and with Keane steering the ship, it usually was.

In total, Keane played 67 times for Ireland, including at the 1994 World Cup where the team was eliminated in the last 16 by Holland.

In 2013, he made a high-profile return to the international set-up, as assistant manager to Martin O'Neill, and at the time of writing they have made reasonable progress with an Irish squad that looked down in the dumps prior to their appointment. The team qualified for the 2016 European Championships, where the drive and passion of the management seemed to spur the side to the last 16 stage. There, they gave a heartening performance against the eventual runners-up France and bowed out in dignified style.

In the tournament, the curtain also came down on the fantastic international career of Robbie Keane, who was the team captain in France.

Robbie Keane first moved to England in 1997 to sign for Wolverhampton Wanderers and although there was always great hope for his future, particularly after his involvement in Ireland's various underage successes, perhaps not even Keane could have imagined the career he would achieve.

He quickly made an impact for Wolves (who always appear to keep a close eye on the youth market in Ireland) and the impish striker impressed everyone in the club by scoring twice on his first-team debut.

After 24 goals in 67 appearances, he received his big break in the Premier League, remaining in the Midlands to join Coventry City for £6m and becoming the most expensive teenager in the history of English football. Unfazed by the (then) hefty price tag, Keane again marked his debut with a brace of goals and his 12 goals for the season certainly made the Dubliner a fairly coveted prospect.

There had been much speculation linking Keane to some of England's biggest clubs, but surprisingly his next transfer was not to one of England's most glamorous sides. Instead, he moved to Italy to join Inter Milan for £13m.

Although I, like many others, felt that the move came too soon for Keane, I could also see why Inter Milan had been keen to acquire his special set of individual skills. For despite the Italians' strong tradition for resolute defending, they are also in love with the role of the so-called *trequartista* or *fantasista*, or the Number 10, as it might be called these days.

Players like Francesco Totti and Gianfranco Zola are idolised in their country for an ability to drift effortlessly into pockets of space between the opposition defence and midfield, to create disorganisation in the rival ranks and to set up goalscoring chances with intricate through passes, or find a shooting chance for themselves by dancing past a series of tackles.

These players are the brains of the attacking operation; the special ones with the nous to find ways through when the defensive door appears firmly shut. In Italy, they are adored by the masses and feared by the rugged defenders who are programmed to keep things tight.

And Keane more or less fitted that bill; a devilishly clever attacker capable of drifting away from his marker and conducting the orchestra from slightly off the front-line.

Yet, equally, the Italians would also have seen, from scouting him in England, that Keane was a deadly penalty box finisher.

Nonetheless, you have to wonder was Keane's Italian adventure really advisable? For despite being financially rewarding, he always faced a remarkably tough challenge to establish himself in the starting team, especially with a deluge of attacking talent in the Inter ranks, including that of Ronaldo, the great Brazilian striker, and Christian

Vieri, not to mention other able deputies like Alvaro Recoba and Hakan Sukur.

Indeed, when the manager who signed him (Marcello Lippi) was dismissed just one game into the new season, Keane's chances of breaking into the side had almost completely evaporated.

Ironically, Lippi's successor was Marco Tardelli, a hero from Italy's 1982 World Cup-winning side, who later featured in the Ireland coaching set-up under Giovanni Trapattoni.

Tardelli, however, would give Keane few opportunities to prove himself and in the end he left Italian shores after a mere 14 appearances and three goals. Luckily for Keane, there was an Irish manager (David O'Leary) at Leeds United, who were fast emerging as a young side of some repute.

With O'Leary publicly showing his admiration for Keane's style of play, he decided to join the Elland Road revolution, initially on loan in December 2000. Keane would net nine goals in 14 matches and his transfer was made permanent in May 2001, as Leeds paid £12m to Inter.

Having signed permanently, Keane showed flashes of brilliance and was a popular figure with the Leeds supporters. Yet he often found himself on the bench, competing with strong figures like Robbie Fowler and Mark Viduka. And so, he largely failed to replicate the form from his loan spell. Then, as the Yorkshire club crashed into grave financial difficulty and was forced to sell its main assets, Keane joined Tottenham Hotspur for £7m, taking the amount of money paid for Keane's services to £38m – and he was still just 22 years old.

Keane would spend six years with Tottenham, where he finally found a place to settle in the long term, and scored 107 goals in 254 appearances, as well as helping them win the League Cup.

'Rather like David Ginola, Keane arrived at a time when Spurs were desperately looking for something; for someone who could conjure magic from nothing,' says Anthony Lombardi, the editor of Tottenham blog 'The Fighting Cock'.

'He was the perfect fit, as we [Tottenham fans] are obsessed with the maverick, the individual, and players we can't pigeonhole. I put Keane third on a list of Tottenham's best strikers in the last 20 years and his greatest strength was the instinctive nature of his play and unpredictability. He helped drag Tottenham up the table to within Champions League qualification,' said Lombardi.

At the time, Tottenham Hotspur were not among the title chasers in the Premier League and were generally labelled as an entertaining but somewhat flaky side, who lacked for a real backbone. They could be very pleasing on the eye but porous in defence, and lacking real leadership when the going got tough. They always had good players, who thrived when Tottenham could turn it on. But because of Tottenham's standing at the time, for Keane to say that he really did represent one of England's genuine giants, he had to look elsewhere.

So, in his pursuit to add a Premier League medal to his collection, Keane made a move to Liverpool in 2008, as another £19m changed hands for his signature.

But despite the Anfield side's large investment, the manager Rafael Benitez only used Keane sparingly. And after a fairly rough period, where the critics came out in force to condemn Keane's Anfield efforts, he eventually returned to Tottenham for £13m, after 28 appearances and seven goals for Liverpool.

Now, Liverpool have not won the Premier League since its inception in the 1990s. But the club's stature and overall reputation in European football remains extremely strong; fuelled enough by past success to see them remaining universally supported (and thus an extremely wealthy club). So, Keane could not be criticised for making the move. It had offered him an opportunity to play in one of the game's great arenas, where plenty of Irish players flourished before him. But it just never worked out.

By 2009, when Keane returned to Tottenham Hotspur, the cumulative transfer fees paid for Keane amounted to approximately £75m. He spent a couple of seasons with Tottenham but was then loaned to Celtic and West Ham United before moving to LA Galaxy in 2011.

Internationally, Keane made a sterling impact, debuting in 1998 and achieving the first of 68 international goals – a record for an Irish player – against Malta in 2000. He played a key role in the 2002 World Cup, scoring an iconic late equaliser in a drawn group match against Germany and converted a high-pressure penalty in the last 16 match against Spain.

In 2004, Keane overtook Niall Quinn as the country's leading goalscorer, reaching 22 goals from 53 appearances, a staggering tally considering that it took Quinn 92 games to amass the previous 21-goal record. Now, Keane and Quinn were very different players; Keane a master of finding space in the box and putting the ball away, and Quinn more of a target man, who worked well in the company of a more mobile strike partner.

Yet Quinn, for durability and longevity, has to be one of the greatest Irish success stories in English football in the last few decades. He was a player who made the very best of his qualities. He never dwelled on what he couldn't achieve on the pitch. Instead, he utilised his aerial prowess and physical strength to forge a good career, proving to young Irish players that you don't necessarily have to be the most naturally gifted player to make your way in the game.

Quinn made his first-team debut for Arsenal in 1985, aged 19, and marked the occasion by netting against Liverpool.

'I got in for the game against Liverpool. Then United. Then Spurs. I got 18 games on the spin. I could have gone to Port Vale and never been heard of again. This is an unbelievable life you know. You've always got to be grateful for it,' says Quinn, who remains the last Irish player to make a lasting impact with the Gunners.

Despite never being the most prolific striker for the club, Quinn was liked by the Arsenal supporters. For he had a selfless approach on the field; always willing to put a shift in and seemingly getting as much pleasure from assisting in a goal as he did from scoring one himself. To the supporters who parted with their hard-earned cash to watch their team play, such qualities, while not in the Liam Brady or John Giles mould, will always be quite endearing.

But despite starting in the 1987 League Cup Final win against Liverpool, Quinn would soon become a fringe player, and when Arsenal won the league in 1989, he fell short of the number of appearances needed to earn a medal.

All told, Quinn enjoyed a reasonable career for Arsenal, scoring 14 goals in just under 70 appearances. But when Alan Smith arrived from Leicester City to become a firm favourite of manager George Graham, Quinn's first-team chances had become less frequent. And in 1990, he signed for Manchester City for £800,000.

Four years earlier, Quinn had made his Ireland debut in a mini-tournament in Iceland and in the summer of 1990, he scored a most memorable goal at the World Cup in a 1-1 draw against Holland.

Quinn also came close to scoring in the quarter-final defeat against Italy when a well-timed header, a trademark of Quinn's playing style, was saved by Walter Zenga.

Back in England, he quickly found his feet at Maine Road (the former home of Manchester City) and in his first full season found the net 22 times – his highest ever return in England's top division.

City finished fifth in both of Quinn's first two seasons at the club but in November 1993, he sustained a bad knee ligament injury which ruined his dream of playing in the 1994 World Cup in the United States.

Quinn has since claimed that he actually returned to a decent level of fitness before the tournament and wanted to be included in the Ireland squad, but that his chances of selection were scuppered by then City chairman Francis Lee, who put his foot down on the issue and refused to allow one of City's best assets to risk aggravating the injury in the rigorous surrounds of the World Cup.

In his absence through injury, Manchester City started to flounder in the league, as they finished in 16th position in the 1993/94 campaign. 'It hit me when I went to get back in the first team the next season. Uwe Rösler and

Paul Walsh had done well. They were the crowd favourites and had kept us up the year before. I was on the bench for at least ten games of that season right at the beginning. Everything was changed. From being top man and going to the World Cup to this,' Quinn recalls in a 1997 interview in *The Irish Times* newspaper.

Quinn would only return to action in the following season, as City – by then on a major downward spiral – narrowly avoided relegation.

At that stage Quinn was supposedly on the verge of joining Portuguese side Sporting Lisbon for almost £2m, but the transfer never happened and, despite reported interest from Everton, he would remain a City player until they finally succumbed to relegation in 1996.

In total, Quinn managed over 200 appearances for City, scoring 66 league goals, before transferring to newly promoted Sunderland for £1.3m.

In his 2002 autobiography, Quinn says that he learned his trade at Arsenal but only really 'became a footballer' at Manchester City. He spoke about his passion for both clubs but claims that everything changed, in his eyes, when Sunderland got under his skin.

His passion for Sunderland would develop in over six years playing for the north-east club, where initially it didn't start so well, as another serious knee injury restricted Quinn to 12 league appearances in the 1996/97 season.

With him sidelined, Sunderland suffered relegation to the second tier but Quinn bounced back to score 14 times in the 1997/98 season, as Sunderland were beaten, agonisingly, in the First Division (second tier) end-of-season play-off final.

Sunderland would return to the top flight after promotion in 1999 with Quinn netting 18 goals in the promotion campaign. He also found the back of the net 14 times as Sunderland, under the management of Peter Reid, finished their first season back in the Premier League in a respectable seventh place.

They also finished seventh in the following season, as Quinn developed a perfect little and large strike partnership with Kevin Phillips, who benefited hugely from many Quinn flicks and knock-downs, and the duo managed 30 league goals between them in the 1999/2000 season before Quinn's playing career concluded in 2002, having scored 61 goals in just over 200 matches for Sunderland.

With Sunderland staying close to his heart, Quinn's relationship with the club did not finish there and he returned to the Stadium of Light in 2006 as a key player in the Drumaville investment consortium that bought the club. The Drumaville consortium acquired a controlling stake in the club and Quinn quickly became chairman, juggling the role for a short period with first-team managerial duties.

Quinn, however, had never intended on being in the dugout. It was a temporary measure as the new owners searched for a long-term replacement for former Ireland defender Mick McCarthy.

Quinn would soon step aside to make way for Roy Keane, who subsequently masterminded a stunning turnaround in Sunderland's form, leading to promotion to the Premier League.

Quinn served as the Sunderland chairman until 2011 when he was replaced by Ellis Short, and then operated as the club director of international development, a position he occupied until early 2012.

For the Sunderland supporters, Quinn ranks highly in the list of all-time heroes and Martyn McFadden, editor of *A Love Supreme,* the popular Sunderland fanzine and website, says: 'As a player, Quinn made a huge impact and became a club hero. He developed a brilliant partnership with Kevin Phillips and was a massive part of the side for several years.'

Such is the adoration for Quinn that McFadden and his colleagues at *A Love Supreme* would record and release, quite successfully, a song in honour of the Irishman.

It was called 'Niall Quinn's Disco Pants', based on a chant initially invented by the Manchester City fans but later adopted by Sunderland as their own.

Quinn would receive an honorary MBE (member of the Most Excellent Order of the British Empire) in 2003 for contributions to football, the community and English charities, and has also established a career in co-commentary/punditry on Sky Sports.

Quinn also has several business interests and has been involved in horse racing management. In addition, in a gesture seemingly indicative of his giving nature, Quinn donated the proceeds from his 2002 testimonial, a match between Sunderland and Ireland, to the Royal Infirmary in Sunderland and Our Lady's for Sick Children in Dublin. Ireland won the match, 0-3, with more than 35,000 people watching on.

It was also roundly reported that, while the chairman of Sunderland, Quinn footed an £8,000 taxi bill in ferrying a large group of Sunderland supporters back home after they were ejected from a scheduled flight from Bristol airport. The supporters, it was reported, had spotted the Sunderland team and Quinn, the chairman, in the airport, and began singing about Quinn. They were then refused entry to the flight but Quinn, unhappy at the treatment of the supporters, refused to board the plane and instead ordered a large fleet of taxis and minibuses to return the supporters to Sunderland.

'That was typical Quinn,' says Martyn McFadden.

'I remember meeting him for the first time when he became the chairman. Now, I am not a shirt and tie guy but decided to go against my better judgement for the meeting. When I entered Quinn's office, he was in a T-shirt and jeans, with his feet on the desk! For our second meeting he took me for a pint of Guinness. That was Quinny, he's a great person. He took over as chairman at a difficult time but put us back on the right path. Thankfully, his comeback, as chairman, never turned sour.

'You look at Alan Shearer's return to Newcastle as manager and they got relegated. Look at Stuart Pearce at Forest, where it went wrong. Sometimes, your legacy gets tainted when you go back but Quinn's sound stewardship of the club ensures he remains a very popular figure at Sunderland,' adds McFadden.

For Ireland, Quinn was a regular fixture in the squad for almost 15 years, appearing in the 1988 European Championships and the World Cups in 1990 and 2002.

Along the way to becoming the team's all-time leading goalscorer (until Robbie Keane took the mantle), Quinn scored some vital goals, including a crucial equalising goal against Holland at the 1990 World Cup that secured Ireland's progress to the last 16. He also scored a memorable goal against England at Wembley Stadium in a 1992 European Championships qualifier.

His 21st goal for his country, against Cyprus in October 2001, set a new goalscoring record for the Irish side and Quinn, indeed, served his country with class and distinction before retiring after 92 appearances.

Now, Quinn would probably be the first to admit that he never possessed the same technical qualities as most players mentioned in this chapter. Still though, he was an honest player who never gave less than his level best. And he played for Arsenal, remember, a genuine giant of English football. That fact will never change.

But what has undeniably changed is the relevance of Irish players to the top clubs featured in this chapter; the likes of Arsenal, Liverpool and Manchester United. Because from a position of Irish players standing shoulder to shoulder with the real elite in Europe and beyond, where they created wonderful sporting memories, the country's current leading players are merely making up the numbers in England's top division.

But how has this become the case? And why are Irish players not overcoming the various obstacles put in the way by England's academy system, to eventually force a way through to playing first-team football?

In the next chapter, I will look inside the walls of that system to see what challenges are facing Ireland's most promising kids and to learn if the success rate in England stands any chance of changing in the future, to ultimately aid the cause of the international team.

Chapter 3

Inside the Walls

THEY pack their bags and fill their heads with dreams. And off they go; the teenage players of Ireland, vying to become millionaire stars in the English Premier League.

Aged just 16 or 17, each and every one has sky-high expectations. They cannot wait to get started alongside their new academy colleagues, as they take the first steps on the road to possibly earning a professional contract.

They are, in many ways, already in a dream world and within minutes of arriving at their port of call, avail themselves of the countless perks that go with joining a top English club: the free accommodation, the food and drink, the sports gear and the social standing of being a footballer. And that's before we even mention the healthy bank balance, which is not always immediate but usually ticks over rather nicely (and rapidly) as the months and years go by.

But it's not long before these players, full of beans and eagerness, have the rug pulled from under them.

For life in England's cutthroat academy system is far from a stroll in the park.

Indeed, what these young players quickly find is that training, unlike at home where they lorded over their peers, is brutally hard and incessantly demanding. Here, they soon encounter professional coaching staff for the first time: goal-setting, highly driven coaches with insatiable appetites for taking unproven talent and turning it into Premier League material.

These coaches simply don't accept second best. And if a player from Ireland is not physically, mentally and technically prepared for the daily challenges, they are quickly cut adrift and through the exit door. These coaches don't care if you have been capped by Ireland at every underage level. They don't realise how many hat-tricks or man of the match performances you accumulated in the local leagues. They don't care about your reputation. For once you get to England you are just another player, another number, and another youngster whose skills, while admirable, are just as dispensable as the next.

These young players soon realise that being part of a professional club is damned hard work and like nothing they knew before. So, having been a stand-out player in Irish schoolboy football guarantees nothing in the rough and tumble of the English game.

If anything, being so far ahead of one's peers, in Ireland, only means that the shock of the new and the heated competition for places can make it even harder for young Irish boys to find their bearings in English academies.

And it was that shock value and the sheer level of contest encountered having signed for Newcastle United in 1995 that caught the former Bohemians midfielder Jim Crawford by surprise, after the legendary Kevin Keegan signed him for £75,000.

His case was slightly exceptional because, unlike the majority of Irish players who go to England, Crawford's move never came in his teens and instead he blossomed into a fine midfielder by remaining in the League of Ireland until his early 20s.

But having been Newcastle's first signing since the high-profile and controversial sale of leading goalscorer Andy Cole to Manchester United, not even that extra bit of experience could help to smooth the transition from part-time player to a full-time, around-the-clock professional.

'Look, Keegan signed me for the first team but what about my first training session? I was doing runs with Peter Beardsley and Rob Lee. I had watched them on television a few weeks earlier! It was hard going, I can tell you,' says Crawford, who has since become a coach in the Ireland international underage set-up.

'I was a fairly big fish in a small pond in Ireland but soon realised I was just another number at Newcastle. They had some really top players; Les Ferdinand and David Ginola had joined in the same summer and Colombian striker Faustino Asprilla came halfway through my first season. The team showed its talent because Newcastle almost won the Premier League – and should have won it. We had a 12-point lead in January [1996] but Manchester United overtook us in March when we had five defeats in eight matches, and they won the league.

'But we should have been able to see the job through.'

That was, of course, the year when Keegan had his infamous 'I'd love it' meltdown on national TV, as Alex Ferguson's so-called mind games completely rattled the Newcastle boss. By then, Crawford had already found league appearances beyond his reach. In his first two seasons at St James' Park, the American-born midfielder failed to play a single league match. And as much as that boiled down to the immense competition in the squad, it also related to the fact that Crawford had found the going tough, as the step up from the League of Ireland proved too much.

'For a start, the training was totally different; far quicker and way more intense. The competition for places was unbelievable. For example, I thought I was doing well in the reserves and ready to play for the first team, but they went and signed David Batty, a league winner and an extremely experienced England international. Young lads need to know that the step up is huge and that getting into the midfield of a Premier League club is so hard. Lee Clark, for example, was there with me and was a tremendous midfielder, but he found first-team chances thin on the ground. Looking back, of course I got to train and play in top-class facilities and was well looked after, financially and personally, but it's just so hard to make it. And I really don't think Irish players are informed enough about this,' he adds.

Getting there, says Crawford, is just the very start of a gruelling process to try to fit in; to prove to coaches and team-mates that you're good enough to make the grade. But he believes too that many Irish players, who have strolled through schoolboy football, simply find it

84

too difficult in coming to terms with the high standards expected, on a daily basis, in English football.

'It's hard to explain to young fellows who just want to follow the dream. But they really have no idea about the win-at-all-costs and pressurised environment in England. You genuinely couldn't understand that until you get there – and by then it's very difficult to grasp and to succeed,' he says.

Crawford, however, still harbours fond memories of his stint on Tyneside, which came to a conclusion in 1998. He spent about 18 months with Reading before returning to the League of Ireland, knowing he had learned so much from his time in an elite Premier League environment. Perhaps Crawford could ponder how things might have transpired had he arrived at Newcastle in more sedate times; possibly away from the high-powered Premier League and tucked away at a level below.

But yet, you regularly see that young Irish players have declined offers from bigger and more elite clubs to sign for a lesser light, like Charlton Athletic or Millwall, for example. And still, despite choosing less glamorous surrounds in the hope (understandably) that it's easier to get in the Millwall team than that of Liverpool or Manchester United, most of these players usually find that it's equally difficult to make a mark, whether it's at Anfield or Aldershot. And they ultimately return home, like Crawford did, with plenty of lessons learned and pleasant memories but nothing tangible to show for their efforts.

You see, regardless of whether you join the Premier League champions or the League 1 chumps, the odds of earning a professional contract at the end of the initial two-year academy scholarship are extremely slight, with one respected Irish schoolboy coach suggesting to me that it's fortunate if one player out of every 20 that goes to England eventually plays regular first-team football.

'The biggest difference is between the development, from a young age, of the Irish and English players,' says the former Arsenal youth player Shane Tracy.

'In England, their players are going to train in Premier League academies from seven or eight. They go for a few nights a week after school and that head start gets them used to the system and what's required, giving them a real advantage over Irish kids who arrive at 16 or 17,' adds Tracy, who realised a dream move to Arsenal close to his 16th birthday in 2005.

There, the Limerick native played in the same team as future Arsenal first-teamers like Nicklas Bendtner, Kieran Gibbs and Alex Song, the latter of whom went on to play for Barcelona. But having only ever played for local schoolboy club Wembley Rovers, Tracy was asked to do a whole host of new things in London.

'Right from the start you're required to maintain the highest level of professional standards, even at a young age,' he says.

'Arsenal, as a club, are keen on high disciplinary standards and the rules have to be kept. Looking back, I understand why they were hard on us. It's the start of your career and they're determined to put you on the right path and get you in good habits. In any professional environment you have to conduct yourself properly and Arsenal, to be fair, was a great place to learn that side of the game.'

The hectic training schedule quickly caught up with Tracy. Like his academy colleagues, he worked under the keen eye of former Arsenal and Ireland great Liam Brady, who for almost 20 years steered the wheel in the Arsenal youth set-up until retiring in 2014.

'The weekly schedule was nearly always the same,' he recalls.

'We got picked up every morning near our digs and brought to the training ground. Monday morning was college for two hours and then lunch and training at 2pm, or you might be involved that night with the reserves, if you were lucky. Tuesday and Thursday was training for two and a half hours from 10am and then you went home or did a double session in the afternoon. That depended on the coach but it was often our hardest day. Wednesday was college all day and used as a rest day. On Friday, we had a quick training session, usually for 75 minutes, to prepare for the game on Saturday. And Sunday was yours to do what you liked. But it wasn't easy and took plenty of getting used to,' he explains.

Tracy would never manage the breakthrough from Arsenal's massively competitive and multinational academy and left the club with six months remaining on his contract. A disappointing campaign in the 2006 FA Youth Cup, he says, led Arsenal to invest heavily in new academy talent, and he felt that his chances of playing regular youth and reserve team football had become very limited.

Suddenly, the reserves could call on talented players like Craig Eastmond, Jay Emmanuel-Thomas, Henri Lansbury and Sanchez Watt – all players who hindered Tracy's chances – while the emerging Nacer Barazite, Emmanuel Frimpong, Conor Henderson, Mark Randall and Jack Wilshere ensured that fierce competition existed among a deeply talented pool of vibrant young players.

Ultimately, the recruitment drive helped Arsenal to win the FA Youth Cup and Premier Academy League in 2009, as well as the 2010 Premier Academy League. But it also spelled the end for Tracy.

'In my case the writing was on the wall for a while; I could sort of see my departure coming,' Tracy admits.

'I had time to come to terms with it. And in the end, I really wanted to go home and agreed to an early contract termination. What did I learn about Irish players and their ability to compete in England? Well, Irish players have the same level of talent as the English youngsters. But the coaching systems in Ireland are way behind. That's not having a go at Irish coaches but the facilities and resources (in England) are just so much better. The young English players are training and playing with better players and getting proper coaching from a young age, enabling their talent to progress quicker from a very young age. That's really what we miss in Ireland and our young players, once they go to England, are playing a massive game of catch-up,' he adds.

Tracy was one of those players who aimed high. He joined one of the game's genuine behemoths. But it's a well-known fact that Arsenal, despite having a few close calls and being a club with strong historic links to Irish players, have not produced a long-term first-team player from Ireland since the Frenchman Arsène Wenger took over in 1996, and totally revamped the Gunners' approach to their youth system.

The Dubliner Stephen Bradley, who joined Arsenal in his teens, got as far as captaining the reserve team. But he still never made the magic step up to the senior side.

And in a heartfelt interview with Emmet Malone for *The Irish Times*, Bradley – who now manages Ireland's most decorated club Shamrock Rovers – spoke openly about the perils of playing for a top English club.

'My mother was a single parent, she came from nothing but she negotiated my contracts on her own, which was unbelievable,' he says.

'She got me a very good deal but after that? At 17 it was "here you go, buy yourself a house or a car... or both". You think, "alright". You're 17 and come from Jobstown in Tallaght and you're living in London with your own house and car. It's ridiculous. It's not right, and that's why we fail. People go on about the other stuff, but that's where we need to start. And if we don't, we won't produce the Robbie Keanes or other players.'

In 2005, Bradley – once tipped as the next Liam Brady – returned to the League of Ireland. It was not long after the prodigious Cesc Fabregas had signed for Arsenal, his exceptional skill and desire to succeed immediately leaving Bradley behind in training.

Then, Bradley was the victim of a horrendous violent burglary at his London home when the youngster was stabbed in the head by an intruder who demanded that Bradley hand over a very expensive watch. Bradley thankfully survived the assault that could have ended his life. But he couldn't survive the intense competition in the Arsenal ranks and the same goes for Graham Barrett and Patrick Cregg, who between them managed six appearances for Arsenal's first team, but could never gain a genuine foothold in the side before their departures.

So, to this day Anthony Stokes remains the last Irish-born player to debut for Arsenal; as an 88th-1minute substitute in a League Cup match in 2005. Yet, despite much talk about Stokes being the next great star of Irish football, he too couldn't force his way into Wenger's long-term plans and instead, having sampled first-team football through a series of loan moves, went on to join Scottish club Celtic, where he did quite well.

That Stokes couldn't make the grade was perhaps more surprising than the aforementioned Barrett, Bradley and Cregg, as for years Stokes's natural forward ability was drooled over by observers of Irish schoolboy football. Indeed, mighty expectations were placed on Stokes's shoulders from an early stage, especially when agreeing to join Arsenal (aged 15) thanks to the desire of Liam Brady to achieve his coveted signature.

But sometimes natural ability and flair, which Stokes had in abundance, are not enough to make the grade. Having the right mentality, willingness to listen and learn and to keep improving, and steely determination and nerve, are characteristics not always attributed to multi-skilled young players. But they are some of the key attributes that academy coaches are constantly looking for.

And generally, clubs won't make hasty calls on whether to retain a player or not. Multiple factors, aside from a player's technical and tactical ability and strength and conditioning will be taken into consideration with most clubs adopting a studied and highly methodical approach to making final judgements on a player's next contract or release.

Discipline, on and off the field, are vitally important, and coaching staff constantly monitor their young players in this regard. They analyse their diets, the willingness to carry out instructions and take advice, and their attitudes to colleagues, coaches and club staff.

And their every move and every pass and cross, and every reaction to good and bad developments, are under microscopic inspection in both training sessions and matches. Yet, that's not to say that highly qualified academy coaches will always get decisions right.

Football, as we know, is a game of subjective analysis and opinion and while one coach might not fancy a certain player, a different coach might feel that the same player is capable of wonderful things in the game.

And in an interview with Tony Leen (*the Irish Examiner*) after retiring as the head of Arsenal's Academy, Liam Brady touched on this very subject by saying: 'In recent times I think I could have got Raheem Sterling, if I'd really gone for him, but I didn't go through with that one. I let kids go at 14 who are making a very good living in the game. Players we don't keep often go on and have good careers in the game. It isn't an end [leaving Arsenal]. Okay, he's leaving Arsenal, but clubs are always ringing us saying, "Well, tell us about this fella, and give me a list of the lads who are leaving." That isn't said to soften the blow for the lad, that's the truth. Within weeks, these lads have moved to another academy. I saw a kid – Lewis Grabban – who Norwich City paid around £3m to Bournemouth for. I let that kid go when he was 14. Dwight Gayle, we let him go too. Invariably, when you leave Arsenal, at the very minimum, other clubs will want to take a look at you on trial. It's very difficult releasing young players. You're there, and you know he and his parents are begging for the words not to come out of your mouth. You've got to almost steel yourself for a couple of days and know that it's in the offing. Be strong and decisive, but also kind, compassionate and understanding and give the kid and his parents something to move on with.'

Invariably, some clubs will be better than others in providing alternative routes for players released from their academy.

But the main thing, according to Charlton Athletic's Irish youth coach Anthony Hayes (formerly of Brentford) is that clubs ensure that any player leaving the club is properly looked after in terms of finding a pathway to another career, whether in football or another form of employment.

'Look, there's no other words for it [delivering news of a young player's release]; it's just a horrible day for everyone concerned but particularly for the kid involved and his parents and you have to try to be sensitive to that,' says Hayes.

'Personally, I see it as the worst part of the job because, essentially, the news you're delivering is breaking a kid's heart, it's breaking a family's heart, and that's not something you ever want to do. But what is essential is to offer the kid a good exit route and try to get him fixed up with another club, if that's his wish. Look, we try to be honest with parents and I suppose when you break the bad news it really shouldn't come as a total shock for them. As the season goes on you feed them bits of information about where the kid needs to improve if he wants to be kept on, so I'd imagine that most parents have a fair idea of what's coming when you sit down and say that the boy is being released,' he adds.

Nonetheless, receiving the fatal news can be a most rotten experience. These players are still teenagers, after all. And for their entire lives, they have desired the life of a footballer. And when they sign the initial two-year apprenticeship, it probably feels that all their wildest dreams have come true. But they get stopped in their tracks, massively, when the dreaded news is delivered.

'Getting released from Wimbledon [then a respected Premier League club] was the worst day of my life,' admits Stephen O'Flynn, who spent three years with the so-called Crazy Gang.

'It was hard to understand why I was let go. You start thinking about the amount of hard work and effort you put in and it makes it even harder to deal with,' he says.

'I suppose people thought that I was living the life of Riley in England, but it was bloody hard work. I know things have changed a bit since then and the academy boys don't do the type of stuff that we did, but we really earned our money, which I can tell you was below £50 a week,' he continues.

'I used to get to training at 9.30am to get the goalposts and training kit ready. I had to clean the boots for Kenny Cunningham, the former Ireland international, and Jason Euell and John Hartson. We often did long runs on the A3 motorway and had to clean the toilets and dressing rooms after training. We [the apprentices] would be absolutely knackered after a day's work. There were plenty of downsides and we only got £42.50 a week, as first-year apprentices. What makes it even harder though, is that you're away from family and friends and at 16 it's difficult to adjust to socialising with different people from different cultures,' he adds.

These days, however, English clubs appear far more sensitive to issues associated with young kids living away from home for the first time. And at Burnley, for example, big efforts are made to fight against the possibility of foreign youngsters becoming homesick; a lonely affliction that brought many blossoming careers to abrupt endings.

'From my experience we have no problem with young Irish lads and we have had plenty of them in recent years,' says Pat McKiernan, Burnley's head of education and welfare, a role that brings daily contact with the club's up and coming youngsters.

'They [the Irish apprentices] get the head down and work hard to make a good impression. But we always try our best to look after them. Our boys go home quite regularly, actually. There are so many affordable flights between England and Ireland. Usually, they go home after a match [on Saturday] and return for training Monday morning. Initially, the boys are housed in groups of two and three with one of our "house parent" families, of which the club has six. It's a system that works well and there are never really any negative issues. They all reside close to the ground and we are in constant liaison with "house parents".

'The set-up offers safety to the boys and gives a welcoming home. Being part of a family set-up in the locality gives structure to their lives. Some make it through to the first team and it's great when it happens. But the way we see it at Burnley, is that the ones who don't make it are equally important,' he adds.

To this end, Burnley works in conjunction with the nearby Accrington & Rossendale College, where young players attend two days a week for lessons. The club, says McKiernan, constantly strives to encourage young players to educate themselves away from football and avail themselves of the options provided by the English Premier League Education Department that delivers a programme to support the technical, tactical, physical, mental, lifestyle and welfare development of all academy players.

McKiernan speaks glowingly about the programme, saying that it points clubs in the right direction regarding player education and welfare. But ultimately, he adds, it's very much down to individuals to apply themselves in the classroom.

'All boys are different in their approach to education and that's normal,' he says.

'While some lads are extremely bright and motivated, others won't possess the same level of concentration and application. But even in such cases, the lads are generally compliant with what has to be done as part of the apprenticeship programme,' he adds.

Burnley's Academy, however, does not currently feature among the country's highest ranked academies, as devised through an independent audit process that assesses and marks clubs in the areas of productivity rate, training facilities, coaching, and education and welfare provisions. The audit ranks clubs between Category 1 and 4 (with 1 being the highest).

And at present the list of Category 1 clubs is largely dominated by the country's most wealthy outfits including Arsenal, Chelsea, Liverpool and the Manchester clubs. It also includes, however, the likes of Brighton & Hove Albion, Reading and Wolverhampton Wanderers, and their inclusions in the highest category is credit to their investment and belief in young players, for it costs £2.5m per annum to run a Category 1 Academy.

Sadly, the introduction of categorisation, and several tweaks to rules on how clubs can operate in the scouting and signing of young players, has led to several lower league clubs abandoning their academies since the introduction of the Elite Player Performance Plan (EPPP) in 2011; a long-term strategy introduced by the Football Association, the Premier League and the Football League with the aim of developing more and better home-grown players to aid the cause of England's national team.

That Category 1 clubs, who are almost all very wealthy anyway, receive greater annual financial rewards for attaining Category 1 status (£775,000 per annum) than those in Category 4, who receive £100,000 per annum, seems like a rather unfair set-up to me, and perhaps goes some way to explaining why it's getting harder for lower league clubs to sustain the expensive academy structures.

In the main, there can be little arguing against the claim that the EPPP has played into the hands of the richer clubs, and put a further dent in the battle for smaller clubs to keep their heads above water.

Yet, one has to wonder if they care at the top end of English football? Do you think that the powers-that-be at Chelsea and Manchester United spare a second thought for the financial plight of clubs like Wycombe Wanderers and Yeovil Town, who both disbanded their academies in the wake of the EPPP? Indeed they do not, as they continue to make millions and millions of pounds each year. All the while, they know that the EPPP has abolished the '90-Minute Rule' regarding the signing from other clubs of players aged 15 and under (which meant that players 15 and under could only sign for clubs within 90 minutes of their home), in favour of giving

Category 1 clubs free rein to plunder any club across the land for talented youngsters, potentially for as little as under £5,000.

Indeed, the EPPP has helped make the rich even richer and as a result, any Irish youngster lucky enough to be recruited by Category 1 clubs (which seems less likely now given their freedom in the domestic marketplace) are able to walk into set-ups and facilities that are beyond their wildest dreams, a fact supported by Tom Mohan, who has visited countless academies in the capacity of Irish youth team manager.

'The young lads are living in a dream, they really are,' says Mohan, who spent his entire career as a part-timer in the League of Ireland, togging out in run-down, outdated grounds that were a million miles away from the pristine conditions in English academies.

'Everything is top-class from the medical facilities to strength and conditioning units, the analysis and so on. Basically, academy footballers are treated much the same as first-team players,' he adds.

And in recent years nowhere has this ability to splash the cash on underage structures been more evident than at Manchester City – despite not one single player developed exclusively by the club playing in the City first team since billionaire owner Sheikh Mansour bin Zayed and the Abu Dhabi Group took control of the club in 2008.

Since the takeover Manchester City has won two coveted Premier League titles and the first of them, in 2012, was their first since 1968, so the Sheikh's input in first-team matters is there for everyone to see, as big-money, top-quality stars like Sergio Agüero and Yaya Toure have come to steer City to glory.

But what's not so obvious is the phenomenal impact that Sheikh Mansour and his associates have had behind the scenes.

For in 2014, City wowed observers of youth football development with the opening of the state-of-the-art City Football Academy, which cost £200m to construct and is rated as arguably the best and most modern academy in Europe. The City Academy is everything that one expects from a project funded by Sheikh Mansour – extravagant, detailed and built to the highest standards. The facilities are simply jaw-dropping and if one is lucky enough to receive a guided tour of the vast facility, located near City's Etihad Stadium, they should take the chance with open arms.

Following its opening, City's Argentine defender Pablo Zabaleta said the club has no excuses for not establishing itself as a major powerhouse in world football. And the former Manchester United star Paul Scholes, speaking as a United supporter, expressed concerns that City's focus on youth development – not only the opening of the academy but also their work locally in recent years – could put them ahead of traditional rivals United in the hunt for young players from in and around Manchester. This despite the fact that United themselves pumped £25m into revamping the Carrington training complex with the addition of a state-of-the-art medical centre and sports science department.

But at City, the bar has been well and truly raised and the 18-acre site boasts 16 outdoor pitches and a main academy stadium with the capacity for 7,000 spectators. There are a further 14 playing surfaces and two half-size pitches that are used exclusively for goalkeeping training. In the first-team building (also part of the overall complex) there are three gymnasiums, an ultrasound room, physio and massage rooms, and a hydrotherapy area with six pools. Above the impressive changing room area is a players' lounge, where young players want for little and are able to kick back and relax after training, and avail themselves of multiple giant flat-screen televisions and computer terminals, as well as pool tables and a refectory where players eat before and after training. Then, a spacious auditorium is utilised by coaching staff for video analysis, and adjacent to the players' lounge is the club's Player Care Department, where young players, who might have some personal worries, can retire to. High among the priorities in this department is the promotion of good ethics and behaviour, including making young players aware of the dangers of drugs, alcohol, gambling and the misuse of social media. The third floor of the first-team building, meanwhile, is used for residential purposes and where the City squad stays overnight before home games. There are 32 en suite bedrooms for the players and the coaching staff and they are all kitted out with specifically made beds and blackout blinds.

With such grand facilities at their disposal, one could expect City to be churning out player after player in the next few years. But so far, there have been very few signs that the club's enormous investment in the youth system is going to pay off.

In City's defence, they had their finger on Ireland's pulse in recent times and have managed to produce players such as Stephen Elliott, Willo Flood, Stephen Ireland and Glenn Whelan. Aside from Stephen Ireland though, who played almost 150 Premier League games for

City, those players have mainly earned their professional stripes at other clubs, with Whelan, most notably, a firmly established top-flight performer for Stoke City.

Furthermore, having signed Whelan from Cherry Orchard, in Dublin, City established firm scouting links with the Dublin schoolboy outfit in 2007, leading to the acquisition of Orchard's left-sided defender Tyreke Wilson in 2013. He signed a three-year professional contract in 2016 and could be one to keep an eye on in the coming years. Yet Wilson will be fully aware of how things turned out at City for Jack Byrne and Ian Lawlor, who were two highly rated youngsters when they moved to Manchester but now find themselves operating at new clubs below the Premier League.

Due to City's extreme levels of wealth and transfer clout, those players were faced with a gargantuan task to break into the first-team picture. Sadly, we might never find out whether Byrne, for example, had the ability to sustain his career in the Premier League. And with City competing for titles at home and abroad, the likelihood is that their managers will always opt for experience over untried youths. Indeed, manager Josep Guardiola intimated as much after Patrick Roberts – on loan at Celtic from City – scored against his parent club in the UEFA Champions League in late 2016.

'We try to help our young players play every single week to see how they are going to develop. Then in the end you have to take a decision. If we are going to try to fight with the big clubs in Europe, to do that is not easy. Young players have to play regularly,' says Guardiola.

His comments suggested that the likes of Byrne and Lawlor had been unlikely to get any sort of lengthy first-team exposure under his guidance. And yet, Guardiola and City are far from the only club that seems hesitant in giving youth a chance.

'Look, we all know it's every player's dream to be a professional in England. They develop the dream from eight, nine and ten years old. And then, all they want is to play for Arsenal, Liverpool and Manchester United. These days it's Chelsea and Manchester City, too,' says Tom Mohan.

'They only realise in their teens just how hard it is to get signed by English clubs. But by then, people have been tipping them to play in England and they get their hopes up, which is a dangerous thing. There is such fierce competition in England because clubs basically have a free market in terms of signing players from across the world. Most Irish kids who get signed are signing two-year scholarships but a very small percentage progress further. It's a really small number who make the grade, it really is. Indeed, I would suggest that we [Irish people] would be better off setting more realistic targets for our young players, and to not place so much emphasis on getting to England. Okay, if it happens then all well and good. But the most important thing, if young players are going, is that they choose the right club that puts plenty of emphasis on promoting young players into the first team,' he adds.

But what top clubs are best promoting such an ethos?

Well, everyone has become very aware about Southampton's ability to push its better young players into the first team with the likes of Wayne Bridge, Calum Chambers, Adam Lallana, Alex Oxlade-Chamberlain, Luke Shaw and Theo Walcott coming through the Saints

Academy to seal massive transfers to some of the leading clubs.

And that's before mentioning their most famous academy product, the Real Madrid and Wales star Gareth Bale, who became the second youngest player to represent Southampton (after Theo Walcott) when he made his debut in 2006. He later transferred to Tottenham Hotspur, where his outstanding ability came to the fore before moving to Madrid for colossal money.

That Southampton have been able to continuously sell their greatest home-grown talent and still hold their own in the top tier is a glowing endorsement of the club's scouting and recruitment departments, as they somehow continue to unearth really able signings (some previously unknown in England) to combine well with the latest batch of academy products.

Their 'produce and sell' policy has served Southampton well in the last decade or so with millions of pounds coming into the club, which then enables reinvestment in the first team and the academy.

Presently, they are the leaders of the pack in terms of giving opportunities to academy prospects, a fact acknowledged and appreciated by Arsenal manager Arsène Wenger, who has praised the Saints' approach in recent years.

'They [Southampton] have certainly been the most prolific producers of top talent in England in the last 15 years. And they have not only produced talent, but top talents,' Wenger notes.

'We have some examples at our club. But don't forget they also produced top quality players like Gareth Bale, Adam Lallana and of course others,' he adds.

Despite not blooding any Irish youngsters in a long time, Arsenal have been among the front-runners for fielding academy players in recent years, with Tottenham Hotspur and Manchester United also holding their own in that respect. Everton, too, have invested heavily in their underage set-up and boast an immaculate academy facility at Finch Farm.

But generally, the bigger clubs are inclined to reach the chequebook, if and when they need to fill a void in the first team. They go for the option of splashing out millions of pounds, generally on foreign imports on high weekly wages instead of looking within.

And it's those extravagant wages and the pitfalls it can lead to that stand at the heart of the failure of many academy players to reach their potential, says the former Arsenal reserve captain Stephen Bradley.

'I knew what I was getting [at Arsenal] but it never really hit home until I turned 17 and went and checked my bank. You go and check and next of all [you're thinking] "How many zeros, how do I count that, like?" That's what it is; straightaway you think "alright, I'll go and buy this, I'll go and do that, I'll go and do that". You forget about what you're there for. You're there to make a career, be a professional footballer. But you don't give a s**t because you have the money. You think you have the money,' he says.

But money – very big money – has changed football beyond recognition in the last few decades with players – thanks in no small part to the Bosman ruling – having the real upper hand over clubs, or indeed over potential new employers when it comes to negotiating contracts, wages, bonuses and signing-on fees.

Like it or not, football agents are now at the heartbeat of the game and its transfer market, and that doesn't just apply to senior football. The agents are all over youth football, in Ireland and England, fearing that they could miss out on the next big thing, who ultimately could make them millions of pounds in the future. And their heavy involvement, it seems, is causing complications.

The kids have never had so many options in a market largely driven by agents and money. Whereas in the past young players and their parents/guardians could opt for the club with the strongest reputation and a track record for producing first-team players from their academy, they are now being pushed and pulled every which way in the market, as agents try to convince them that accepting the strongest financial offer is what makes sense, rather than ensuring that youngsters go to clubs that provide tried and trusted pathways to the first-team action.

This is where the parents need to stand up and be counted, and you would hope that most parents are strong enough, in these difficult circumstances, to put their foot down and ignore the pound signs to get their son into an academy that suits his skills and caters for future development, both on the pitch and in the classroom.

'But it's not always that easy,' says Liam Brady. 'Player and parent power has come to the fore over the last four or five years,' he admits.

'Because of the competition at the very top of English football and the money that's involved – the money gets into youth development as well – there is huge competition. Whereas in 1996 and for ten years, it was all about persuading the parents and the boy that the club was right for him, now you can have a boy at your club from the age of eight, and then he can say, "I've got a better offer from somewhere else," so that creates a whole new set of issues to deal with. You've got agents who are giving the parents another side of the story – the financial bottom line – so that's made it much more difficult.

'Also, the system in England has become a lot more bureaucratic – they've created this categorisation of clubs and academies. Arsenal has got to be in Category 1 because, well, it's Arsenal. To be a Category 1 club, you've got to have huge numbers of staff, huge amounts of previewing, reviewing, assessment – and it's all got to be logged. Boxes to be ticked. That's not the job that I came into. No decision is made in five minutes any more. There are negotiations with the agent, then the agent comes back and more talks ensue. I always used Arsène Wenger when it came to the crunch over whether we wanted to get a particular player from outside, or one of our players who was having his head turned. In that, he'd be a tremendous help.'

While digesting those remarks, it seems likely that Brady had become somewhat disillusioned at the way that youth football is headed. It's just an entirely different world to when Brady had moved to Arsenal in the 1970s – around the same time that fellow Dubliner Don O'Riordan was snapped up by Brian Clough for Derby County, who had been English champions in 1972 and 1975.

Unlike many modern academy players, O'Riordan lived a very simple and admirable lifestyle before making his top-level debut in 1977, as Derby drew 0-0 against Tottenham Hotspur.

'Back then it was different and training and playing games was all that mattered,' says O'Riordan, who also played professionally for Preston North End (under the management of 1966 World Cup winner Nobby Stiles), Carlisle United, Middlesbrough, Grimsby Town and Notts County (including in the top tier for the latter until injury prematurely ended the experience).

He remembers, for example, running back to his digs, 'a fair distance' from Derby's training ground, to write a letter to his parents about the thrill of training, for the first time, with County stars Archie Gemmill and Roy McFarland.

'We didn't have a phone in the family home in Ballyfermot [Dublin], so writing was the only way to make contact. It was long before mobile phones. Yeah, I remember running back to my digs. I cramped up a couple of times but couldn't stop. I had to get the words on a page to say how fantastic it was to be in the company of so many top players,' O'Riordan recalls.

These days, I wonder if young players have that kind of enthusiasm and almost childlike love for the game? It surely exists in some. But when you see young academy graduates pushing to join bigger clubs after five or ten first-team games for the club that helped them along, it does make you ask whether some academy kids, as well treated as they are, are simply losing passion for the sport and the desire to help the club that nurtured them once more esteemed clubs with deeper pockets – and more lucrative contracts to offer – start sniffing around.

To this end, O'Riordan feels it's imperative for aspiring footballers to keep their feet on the ground, though he also insists that doing that is probably harder than ever before.

'What advice would I give young footballers? Well, I always preached about the importance of dedication to your sport and self-discipline,' he says. 'Look, I used to get slagged and called boring because I didn't go drinking with the English lads at Derby. Believe me, it was probably tempting from time to time because you were homesick and down. But why do anything that could reduce the odds of getting a professional contract? Why would you do that – having spent all your life striving to be a footballer? So, you need to have strength and stick to what is right. And it pays off when the contracts are handed out. It's also important for players to take advantage of the education provided.

'When I was over there I didn't pay much heed to lessons. I didn't want to know about carpentry. There were lads who felt the same but then they didn't make it in football and were left with nothing – no football career and no options outside. With the percentage of Irish lads breaking into first-team football dropping all the time, you have to ensure that this doesn't happen to you. Do your stuff in training and in matches and behave away from the club, but don't neglect your study either because you don't know what's around the corner, as a footballer,' says Don.

Indeed, it is surely difficult to predict where someone's career might be in six months' time, let alone ten years down the road, meaning that O'Riordan's qualified views should be taken seriously by any young Irish player contemplating England.

Over there, everything will be done to hone you into a fine footballer and upstanding young person. You will be treated extremely well, in most cases, but will also operate in a highly pressurised, ultra-competitive environment that never settles for second best. You need to have strong self-belief, courage and a never-say-die attitude. And you need to be able to take the knock-backs.

But if you still don't believe how the great English dream can become a living nightmare then read on, as the next chapter takes an in-depth and personal look at the turbulent ways in which the professional ambition and hopes and dreams of many young Irishmen have fallen asunder, for a plethora of reasons, in the rough and tumble of English football.

Chapter 4

Home Is Where the Hurt Is

IT was the summer of 2009. Michael Jackson had just died. Oasis and U2 were touring the world and the Irish education system was reeling after the Leaving Certificate English paper was postponed for two days when it emerged students in County Louth had already seen the exam paper.

Neil Yadolahi, meanwhile, one of the most exciting prospects in Irish football, was at a party. The bash was for him. His family and friends had gathered to celebrate Neil's impending transfer to professional football. Neil would spend much of the night shaking hands with relatives; some he knew very well while others were not so well known and played only fleeting roles in his childhood.

Nonetheless, they all gathered to wish him well for his new adventure. His parents, Breda and Saba (the latter originally from Iran), watched on proudly. Their son was on the verge of realising the great childhood dream of millions. Their understandable concern at seeing their 17-year-old son move abroad, to pursue a career in football's highly competitive environs, was soothed by a mutually shared pride and joy.

There was plenty of back slapping as close friends, neighbours and mere acquaintances queued to get a piece of the rising star. Neil felt comfortable and appreciated. The warmth and love in the room was palpable and the sheer anticipation and excitement of the challenge ahead eased Neil's sense of sadness developed from seeing just how many people cared.

He was due to leave Dublin the following morning and embark on a new life across the Irish Sea, having agreed to sign a two-year scholarship deal to play for the English Premier League club, Burnley FC.

The Clarets were on the crest of a wave, newly promoted to the cash-rich Premier League and managed by one of Britain's most exciting up and coming bosses, Owen Coyle, who was born in Scotland but represented the Republic of Ireland (just the once) at senior international level.

Terry Pashley, a respected youth coach with Burnley, was instrumental in persuading Neil to shun interest from Reading and to move to Turf Moor, but Yadolahi also met with Coyle before agreeing to sign and was impressed by the manager's empathetic persona.

Convinced Burnley was the right place to further hone his skills as a central defender, Neil signed for the Lancastrian side. Initially, his decision looked impressive, as the former Templeogue United and St Kevin's Boys player was promoted to the reserve side after just five months' youth team football.

'It went so well that the football covered any lingering doubt about being away from home. It blocked out the homesickness, in a way,' Neil says.

Although not a key factor in how Neil's Burnley career would eventually unravel, Coyle departed the club midway through the 2009/10 Premier League season, joining Bolton Wanderers.

Brian Laws, who later had a brief spell as director of football at Shamrock Rovers, manned the Burnley ship until the end of the season, but couldn't steer them clear of relegation. Neil, however, still believed he could make the breakthrough to Burnley's first team. In fact, he thought that relegation back to the second tier and a less competitive level than the Premier League might even help his cause.

But Neil's problems really began in his third season at Turf Moor. Major injury problems struck – he suffered a grade-two tear in his thigh, which went undiagnosed for two weeks, and then a related grade-two tear to his groin – while his relationship with manager Eddie Howe, appointed in January 2011, was far from smooth.

'There was talk about a one-year extension but in the end it was better for both parties if I looked for something else,' says Yadolahi.

There were a few offers from English third-tier clubs but Neil didn't feel that dropping down the divisions would do his career much good.

'I wanted to move on from reserve football. I had enough of that with Burnley and didn't think the lower leagues would be much better,' he says.

Like many out-of-contract players, Neil played a waiting game until Derby County – also of the Championship and managed by Nigel Clough, the son of legendary Nottingham Forest and Derby County boss Brian Clough – enquired about his services.

Neil was thrilled to sign for the Rams but a couple of weeks into pre-season he sustained another dreadful injury, this time to his calf and ankle. Completely fed up with the injury-rehab cycle, he approached Clough to request the cancellation of his contract. Clough reluctantly agreed and a few days later Neil was on a plane to Ireland. On this occasion, there was no party – and nobody waiting with open arms at the airport. Neil was alone.

The only person that knew about his return – aside from Derby County FC – was his girlfriend.

'I felt like I had let everybody down. I was really low, in a hole I couldn't see a way out of. I stayed with my girlfriend and locked myself away for two weeks until my mother, God bless her, found out that I was home. Seeing my lifetime dream fade away was heartbreaking and I couldn't handle it. My mother was upset I didn't confide in her, but I felt ashamed coming home. I thought I had let my family down,' says Neil, who soon moved back to the family home.

It quickly became clear that events in England had negatively impacted on Neil's state of mind. After a routine visit to a local barber, Neil's friends told him of two bald patches on the back of his head. At first, he was livid and thought the barber had made a mess of the job. But when the family doctor diagnosed Neil as having alopecia areata, a condition often brought on by stress or trauma, he was at a low ebb.

'Everybody thinks footballers have it all and can't be unhappy, or have anything to complain about. But apart from kicking a ball around a field for a living, footballers are exactly the same as people from other walks of life. They have emotions, feelings and can get dragged down. I told the doctor about my bad experiences at Burnley and Derby, and how I never felt so low. It wasn't the most comfortable conversation but at least after speaking to the doctor I had told someone the way that I felt, and that was an important step,' says Neil.

Yadolahi, who was capped by Ireland at various levels up to Under-19, was prescribed anti-depressants and a cream for the alopecia. He showed tremendous courage and honesty by, firstly, dealing with his problem, and then by speaking publicly on the subject. For someone so young to have the character and mental strength to do so is a credit to the young man.

However, he knew that he was not alone in a football world where it's almost taboo to speak about mental health.

In April 2014, FIFPro, the leading international players' union, revealed that more than a quarter of current professionals suffer from anxiety and/or depression. The statistic came from a study conducted by the international organisation with just over 300 players, past and present, in six leagues, including the League of Ireland.

The study, overseen by Dr Vincent Gouttebarge in the Netherlands, found that 26 per cent of current players suffer from anxiety or depression, while 19 per cent use alcohol in an excessive way. The numbers were significantly higher in most categories for retired players with 39 per cent experiencing anxiety or depression and

32 per cent reporting adverse behaviour with alcohol. The figures were based on responses from players in the Netherlands, New Zealand, Scotland, the USA, Australia and Ireland.

General secretary of the Professional Footballers' Association of Ireland (PFAI), Stephen McGuinness says that a stigma around depression prevents footballers coming forward with their issues.

'Unfortunately, a lot of players are still reluctant to talk and seek help. Sadly, such is the stigma related to depression in sport, footballers probably think that admitting to depression or mental health difficulties will be perceived as a sign of weakness,' McGuinness says.

German footballer Andreas Biermann, for example, revealed his battle with depression in 2009. But in a chilling interview not long after announcing his personal battle, he says: 'If any footballers out there are suffering from depression I advise them to keep it to themselves.'

Biermann was speaking after the club he was contracted to decided not to renew his contract on its expiration. Though there is no evidence to suggest the club's decision was based on Biermann's personal difficulties, the underlying tone of his comment, made in German magazine *Stern*, indicated that his football life was negatively impacted by announcing his problems.

Biermann tragically took his own life in 2014, aged 33, having initially revealed his suffering after the death of Robert Enke, the former German goalkeeper, who also suffered mental health problems before committing suicide in 2009.

The former Leeds and Newcastle United midfielder Gary Speed also took his own life in 2011 after mental health difficulties. He had been managing the Welsh national side at the time, while Clarke Carlisle, a former team-mate of Yadolahi, who went on to become the chairman of the PFA, has spoken in great detail about his battle with depression and alcohol, which, aged 21, had led to a failed suicide attempt that included consuming a heavy dose of painkillers and alcohol on a London park bench. Carlisle also admitted trying to take his own life in 2015.

These are just some of the more highly publicised cases of footballers struggling with their mental health and while Yadolahi battled against his problems, he says: 'Those cases were tragic but the dressing room is not a place to display weakness. I hope this is changing.'

To help the cause, the PFA runs two offices, in Manchester and London, where players can seek advice on mental health. Its head of player welfare is Michael Bennett, a former Charlton Athletic and Millwall player. Bennett oversees outreach and educational work in clubs. And along with a team of counsellors, he endeavours to address a wide range of personal problems.

Speaking in 2015, Bennett says: 'The problems vary a great deal. Often it's the pressure of the game, or not playing, or maybe the manager doesn't like the player. It might be injuries or financial problems or marital problems. It could be gender problems. Usually there is a root issue to problems, so if a player has depression or stress or anxiety there is an issue behind that. And usually when we look at a root issue, we tend to find that the stress, anxiety or depression alleviate.'

The English FA, meanwhile, has highlighted mental health as a key part of its inclusion and antidiscrimination work, and helps to fund the Sporting Chance rehabilitation clinic.

John Bramhall, the PFA deputy chief executive, told me: 'Emotional and mental issues have been very much in the forefront of the PFA's work over the past four or five years and we put in place a network of fully qualified and trained counsellors. All clubs within the leagues have welfare and safeguarding officers who deal with any issues or concerns that both players and parents have. League Football Education also has a virtual learning facility which has a confidential section where players can raise any issues they may have. There is also a network of counsellors available to all PFA members and this concept is a 24-hour helpline in complete confidence.'

With a clearer mind, Yadolahi maintains a desire to succeed. Despite his many falls, he believes he has a career in the game. But once back in Dublin, Neil decided to take stock and stay in Ireland for a while. He needed to be around those he trusted, if only for a few months, and signed a short-term contract with Premier Division Bohemians. He played four games, scoring once, before his contract expired at the end of the 2013 season. He played for a period in Armenia and returned to Irish football before playing for Vancouver Whitecaps, and earning senior international recognition for Iran, his father's birthplace, in 2016.

Still only 23, Yadolahi has plenty of time to crack the professional game and crucially, he possesses many experiences – some good but more bad – that could stand him in good stead in the future.

Whatever football holds for Yadolahi, it was more important to address the mental health issues that arose from his time in England. He did so manfully. And his football skills will hopefully see him prosper in the future. But his story informs us that while football's great big show must always go on, despite the casualties, the party doesn't last forever.

For Kevin Doherty, a strapping centre-back from Dublin, a golden future with Liverpool was derailed not by depression or mental health issues, but by injury.

In the summer of 1999, he was at the centre of the Anfield dressing room. Gerard Houllier was the manager and Irish international Steve Staunton was among a host of established Kop idols, along with England strikers Robbie Fowler, Emile Heskey and Michael Owen; defender Jamie Carragher and midfielder Jamie Redknapp, too. It was a star-studded dressing room.

One day, Doherty took a look around the dressing room and figured, with good reason, that he had 'made it' in football, after being propelled into the first-team squad having impressed Houllier in his debut season at the renowned English club.

'I was only at the club a year but it was obvious Houllier liked me, as a player and a person. I was absolutely delighted when he promoted me to the first-team squad,' Kevin says.

Having starred for the Republic of Ireland schools' side and with Home Farm, Doherty made a dream move to Liverpool in 1998. Aged 18, Kevin went to England at an older age than many of his schoolboy team-mates, who included Richard Dunne (Everton), Barry Ferguson (Coventry City) and Stephen McPhail (Leeds United).

'There was nobody beating down my door in my teens,' he admits.

'Instead, I started getting attention in my Leaving Cert year,' adds Doherty, whose early schoolboy days were with St Michael's in the north Dublin suburb of Donnycarney.

'I was part of a St Joseph's Secondary CBS (Fairview) team that won an All-Ireland Schools' title and was spotted by Noel McCabe, a scout, in the final. Noel sent me to Liverpool. I had trials at Luton Town and Sheffield United but they never amounted to anything. I impressed at Liverpool and agreed to sign for them in April 1998. I did my Leaving Cert before going over. At least I got that done adequately, I would say. But all the while my mind was on playing for Liverpool,' says Kevin.

Doherty's transfer to Liverpool almost hit a last-minute snag. Liverpool's city rivals Everton had an official link with his schoolboy club, Home Farm, which supposedly gave the Toffees first choice on promising Home Farm players. The link had played no small part in Richard Dunne's transfer to Goodison Park. And when Everton got word of Doherty's impending transfer, they were not best pleased.

He explains: 'Everton phoned my house the night before I was supposed to sign. They offered crazy stuff to change my mind. But it was too late. Liverpool had offered a three-and-a-half-year professional deal, which was beyond my wildest dreams, and my heart was set on Anfield. Nothing was going to change my mind – no amount of money. I was going to Liverpool – even had Manchester United, who I supported, come in with a late offer.'

Kevin spent his debut season playing, primarily, for Liverpool's Under-19 side. He also played in a few reserve games. Steven Gerrard, who later became one of

Liverpool's most iconic ever players, was in the same boat, while Doherty occasionally shared the reserve dressing room with the likes of Fowler, Owen and Redknapp.

'It was normal back then and I was never overawed,' he says.

'You get used to the place, particularly if you're playing well and making progress. Steven [Gerrard] was always a special player and a good fella. He had tremendous natural ability and it wasn't a surprise when he established himself in the first team,' says Kevin.

'The whole purpose of going over was to go as far as my ability could take me. I wasn't about to feel awkward because I was surrounded by Premier League players. I knew the boss liked my way of playing and I was feeling good about my chances. Why would I feel inferior when the manager clearly liked me?' he says.

Kevin's life was really good. He liked living on Merseyside. It was similar, in many ways, to living in Dublin. He also felt comfortable in the first-team setting and was ready to challenge more established defenders for a place in the Liverpool side.

Then disaster struck. While on international duty with the Ireland Under-18s, Kevin went in for a routine tackle, from which he didn't emerge well. He broke his femur (thigh bone) – the longest and strongest bone in the body – in his right leg. He wasn't to know it at the time but his career would never be the same again.

'It was a horrific injury and not one you associate with football. Because the femur is so strong, it usually takes a lot of force to break it. The Liverpool physio described it as car crash stuff. In fact, the club doctor started bringing my scans to medical seminars to illustrate to fellow medical professionals the extent of the injury and to discuss ways of dealing with it,' says Kevin.

In a matter of weeks, Doherty says, he went from a potential first-team starter to a medical freak. He spent the next nine months on the sidelines but eventually, after a tortuous rehab schedule, managed a few reserve games in the 2000/01 season.

'I was actually doing okay, I suppose, but then the injury returned. Eventually, I needed a second operation to remove the plate and 12 screws, which kept me out for another eight months. So, that was 17 months missed, nearly a year and a half. It was a disaster,' he says.

In the meantime, Liverpool had spent millions of pounds on central defenders, who understandably moved ahead of Doherty in the pecking order. Unsurprisingly, Liverpool had moved on and the writing was on the wall for Doherty some time before he eventually parted with the club in 2001.

'I knew it was coming for a while. I'd simply had too many injuries and they were really bad ones, from which you rarely come back. I have no bitterness towards Liverpool. They were great and always treated me well. Houllier was a great person and I received plenty of support through my injuries from Brian Kerr and Sammy Lee. But I can't regret my career. I trained and played with top-class players and although I didn't make the ultimate breakthrough, I cherish my time in England,' he says.

Having left Liverpool, there was interest from Blackpool, Grimsby Town and Queens Park Rangers. But a phone call from Dermot Keely, who was running a full-time set-up with Shelbourne, convinced Kevin to return to Ireland. Doherty would spend four years at Tolka

Park before going on loan to Waterford United and then joining Longford Town. His playing days would conclude in 2010 after a spell with Bray Wanderers and another brief stint with Shelbourne. He works as a postman and became the manager of Shelbourne in 2015.

'I look at television and see the players I played with. A lot of them are massive stars – while I'm delivering post in Dublin! But, as I say, there's no bitterness in me,' he says.

However, Doherty also has strong words of warning to young players who return to Ireland after failing to make the grade in England.

'As a manager, I see young lads coming back and they think it's easy to get in an Irish club team. It doesn't happen like that, I'm afraid. I am worried about young players in our country, particularly when you see lads playing in the First Division [the second tier] with player agents [representing them]. I mean, what the hell is that about? Some lads play five or six games in the First Division and think they've made it. They live in cloud cuckoo land,' Doherty says.

There are, unfortunately, many stories like Doherty's, involving players that suffer injury after injury in their youth career in England. In a way, if one fails to become a professional player due to a string of unfortunate injuries, it's almost harder to take than, say, if a player is simply not good enough or doesn't possess the appropriate dedication. These unlucky players are not denied a chance to 'make it' through a lack of skill and/or commitment, and are instead left feeling robbed by their injury struggles, and of the opportunity to showcase their talent at the highest level.

Given its nature as a high-contact sport, football naturally leads to injuries. But in some cases, recurring injuries have led to players either not fulfilling their promise and as a result being forced down the leagues to operate at a lower standard, or, in other more extreme cases, recurring injuries have instigated the early retirement of some promising players. A lengthy list of well-known players immediately spring to mind in this respect. The likes of Dean Ashton, Andy Carroll, Abou Diaby, Kieron Dyer, Duncan Ferguson, Owen Hargreaves, Ledley King, Chris Kirkland and Jonathan Woodgate have all suffered with chronic injury problems in their careers. And although they played at the highest level in England (and in Spain in Woodgate's case), their achievements were undoubtedly restricted by the consistent presence of injury.

Dylan McGlade, a young Irish player, suffered extensively through injuries while with Middlesbrough. Indeed, you almost need a degree in medicine to understand some of the debilitating knocks that he sustained. But the really eye-opening aspect of McGlade's experience in England lies more in the way he was treated by his former club on his release.

'I was only coming out of a period of homesickness, a few months into my two-year contract, when I got the first injury; a really bad knee into my thigh that resulted in myositis ossificans,' he recalls.

Myositis ossificans is, basically, where calcifications (the accumulation of calcium salts in a body tissue) occur at the site of an injured muscle, most commonly in the arms or the quadriceps or the thighs.

'I got really bad bruising… blood coming out of bashed capillaries and then drying up. The calcium formed a kind of bone running the length of my thigh and this kept me out for about three months. I was on crutches and a lot of anti-inflammatory tablets because if it didn't go away a surgical removal would be required,' adds Dylan.

It was an injury that Dylan – then an Under-17 international – had previously never heard of. And it came as a devastating blow after an initial positive start with Middlesbrough.

'It was a terrible pity. I was doing so well,' he says.

'For the first three months as a scholar, I was in heaven. I adjusted quickly and settled in the changing room. After five weeks I played in a reserve friendly and was training with the reserves a couple of times a week. I was starting for the Under-18s and playing well,' he adds.

Dylan, who played schoolboy football for Swords Rovers, Malahide United, Home Farm and Shelbourne, would slowly recover from his injury to return to the Under-18 side. A day before his 17th birthday, he scored his first goal for the club.

'My parents came over for the game against Bolton, so I was over the moon to score. I felt very proud,' Dylan says.

But only three days later, his world collapsed. The Middlesbrough Under-18s were playing against Everton and Dylan ruptured his ankle syndesmosis (where at least one of the ligaments connecting the bottom ends of the tibia and fibula bones – the lower leg bones – is sprained).

That was not all. He also broke bones in his foot and suffered a spiral fracture running all the way up his fibula (the inner long bone of the leg, the shin bone). The injury knocked him for six.

'Recovering from even mild injuries of this type takes at least twice as long as a typical ankle sprain,' Dylan explains.

'It's one of the worst injuries you can get, as it ruptures the ligaments at the front of the ankle, the ones that basically hold together your foot and leg. It resulted in surgery with a metal plate inserted along the side of my fibula and three wires going through my ankle to hold it in place. I found the rehab so hard and lost my cool and my head. It was frustration. I was so desperate to play and to show Middlesbrough what I could do, so missing months of training and playing was extremely hard and completely wore me down,' Dylan says.

Being injured, says Dylan, leads to great anxiety. Injured players, he stressed, are always concerned that missing too many matches will lead the club to become frustrated over the player's lack of availability for selection, and ultimately to purchasing an alternative option for that player's position. It leads to self-doubt, he says, and a diminishing sense of confidence. Very quickly, he adds, you become dispensable.

'I remember returning to Ireland to play for the international side and feeling so depressed about going back,' he recalls.

'I would never tell anybody at the club how I was feeling. At one stage I contemplated booking flights home without the club knowing. The coaches are not stupid and notice when you're not right. There were times I was close to tears in the manager's office, feeling like I had to get home,' he adds.

The manner of Dylan's release from Middlesbrough, in 2013, taught him about the ruthless side of football.

'The day I found out was the most horrible ever. I'd be lying if I said I didn't cry. It felt like the end of the world. My dad flew over because a meeting was arranged with

Dave Parnaby, the head of the academy. He took us to his office and didn't beat around the bush. The first thing he said was that I wasn't getting a professional contract or a third year as a scholar,' he says. (English clubs can offer 'scholarships' to promising young players from the age of 16 and, generally, these are for two, or three-year periods. Thereafter, players will graduate to the reserve team or be 'let go' by their clubs. In McGlade's case, his initial scholarship had been for two years.)

'Despite the injuries, I was stunned. I just sat there in floods of tears. He [Parnaby] said he would phone other clubs about my availability and that he would do everything to find another club in England. His opinion was that I was too talented to play in Ireland. He said that if I matured, I could play at the highest level within five years. I was told I could leave training with my father (it was about 1.30pm) and spend some time with him. For some reason, I felt I still had time, as it was only February, to change their minds, so I started straight away and went back out training. I was so motivated to prove them wrong and that motivation, I suppose, mostly stemmed from anger. But it was all in vain,' he says.

'Middlesbrough didn't really help me. They sorted a trial with Hibernian in Scotland, in March, and there was talk about Swindon Town. But nothing came of it. After the meeting with Parnaby, I never got a chance to show scouts what I was capable of because Middlesbrough continually left me on the bench. I never had contact from anyone at the PFA, the PFAI or the FAI, but probably didn't expect it. It taught me that football is a cutthroat and brutal business. Clubs need to realise that although it's a professional environment, young kids are going to mess up and make mistakes along the way. I never felt the club understood that. My advice to Irish players going to England is to speak to your parents every single night. It releases all the tension and you can have a moan. Sadly, I didn't do that and deeply regret it. You also have to train and play in every game like you're fighting for your life.

'The two years with Middlesbrough went very fast. Sleep is important – you need lots of it. And I regret the days that I sat in my bedroom with only my thoughts for company. It messed me up and left me in worse form. Another thing I hated was not having anything to do on weekends. I suggest getting close to someone over there and organising stuff on weekends to get out of the house. Also, stay behind after training and do little bits yourself or stay in the gym when everyone has gone home. Always look to improve yourself – coaches absolutely love that,' Dylan says.

Upon his release, Dylan would return home to Shelbourne after trials with Burnley and Oxford United. After four games with Shelbourne, he suffered another ankle syndesmosis, this time in his other leg. But he has since recovered to play for another couple of League of Ireland clubs.

There were, unsurprisingly, some major tales of woe in researching this book. But interestingly, it was also fascinating to discover that some players didn't stay in England to be ultimately told that they were not good enough. Instead, they took the decision away from their clubs, deciding to return to Ireland having had enough of the demands of the professional game.

Some, like former Ipswich Town goalkeeper Shane Supple, simply had enough of the lifestyle associated with professional football, while others thought the pressure of constantly reaching for high targets was too much to take.

Football can be all-fulfilling and extremely rewarding, making people happy, both personally and financially, and providing players with glory, widespread acclaim and many fond memories. But during my research, I heard the following words continually used to describe professional football: dog-eat-dog; pressurised; ruthless; shark-infested and ugly.

Strong words to associate with the so-called beautiful game. But when you stand back from the pictures of glamour portrayed in many media outlets – and through the behaviour of some high-profile players – to speak to the more ordinary players, it is obvious that beneath football's surface lies a more regrettable side. And for some players who decided to turn their back on the ugly side of the game, they displayed more character, in many ways, than those who stayed in the game against their better judgement.

Respected US sports psychologist Dr Alan Goldberg, the author of over 30 mental toughness training programmes and books for athletes, says that 'quitting is a so-called dirty word in sport. No one wants to be known as a quitter. No one wants to be labelled the guy who "just couldn't hack it".

'For many,' he adds, 'being called a quitter is the ultimate form of disgrace for an athlete. After all, when the going gets tough, the tough are supposed to get going, right? What's that they say about quitters? That they are taking the easy way out? Perhaps they're wimps, weaklings or softies? Do they lack heart? Are they character deficient? Let's face it, in the world of sports, stick-to-it-iveness is the ultimate secret to success. More so than natural talent, physical advantages or luck, your ability to pick yourself up after a fall, time and time again, to persevere and keep going, is the most important factor in successfully achieving your goals. However, quitting isn't always as bad as everyone says. There are times when leaving your sport is the absolute healthiest thing you can do. Similarly, there are times when continuing to stay is more of a sign of weakness than strength. In fact, sometimes not quitting is flat out self-destructive and stupid.'

Shane Supple was one of Ireland's most promising goalkeepers when he signed for Ipswich Town. Quickly establishing himself at the Suffolk club and playing in the 2005 FA Youth Cup Final win, he was earmarked as a long-term option for the club goalkeeper position.

Subsequently, he made his first-team debut in an English Championship game in 2005, aged 18, as a substitute for the injured Lewis Price. Supple had a substantial run in the side under manager Joe Royle but was unable to firmly nail down the first-choice spot over the next few years, as a succession of senior goalkeepers, including former Arsenal and Everton custodian Richard Wright, were favoured ahead of the young Dubliner.

Supple was loaned to Falkirk in Scotland and to Oldham Athletic in the third tier before eventually – and in sensational style – announcing his retirement, aged just 22. It was a decision that left most observers bemused, including the Ipswich manager, one Roy Keane.

He turned his back on a long-term career in football, convinced that the culture that goes hand-in-hand with being a footballer was not to his taste. Slowly, he says, his

ROY KEANE *Roy Keane, the former Manchester United captain, left Old Trafford in 2005 after a trophy laden career. Will Keane be forever remembered as the last truly great Irish player in the English Premier League?*

MARTIN O'NEILL *The current Republic of Ireland manager cannot call on any players from England's top clubs at present, and wonders if modern young Irish players have lost the ruthless edge needed to make it to the very top.*

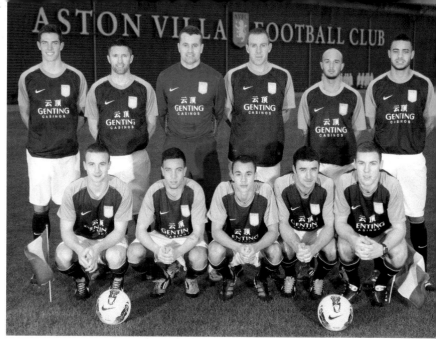

ASTON VILLA IRISH CONTINGENT *There were 12 Irish players on the books at Aston Villa – then a mainstay in the Premier League – in 2012, including a handful of extremely promising youngsters. By 2017, none of the players remained at the club with many dropping into England's lower divisions.*

SHANE SUPPLE *Many young Irish players are dejected when their clubs let them go. The story of goalkeeper Shane Supple, however, is very different, and in this book he recalls the many factors that drove him to leave the professional game in search of genuine happiness.*

BRIAN KERR *A serial winner as manager of Irish youth teams and former senior international boss, Brian Kerr now finds himself somewhat ostracised from the running of football in Ireland. A crying shame, the author argues, in Chapter 6.*

DARYL HORGAN
Daryl Horgan's late ascent to the English game and the senior Irish squad caught the imagination of Irish fans. But could his meteoric rise from the League of Ireland present as a career template for young Irish players in the future?

LIAM BRADY There have been times when Irish players presented as crucial figures in some of England's most successful club sides. Liam Brady was the darling of the Arsenal faithful for many years before embarking on a golden period in Italian football, too.

JIM CRAWFORD Jim Crawford stepped out of the League of Ireland to join Premier League title challengers Newcastle United. In this book, he provides first-hand knowledge about how difficult it is for young Irish players to make the grade at the highest level across the water.

SEAMUS COLEMAN *Seamus Coleman has arguably been Ireland's finest export to the Premier League in the last decade or so and yet, faces the distinct possibility of going through his entire career without winning a single major honour in the English game.*

PAUL McGRATH *A throwback to when the Irish were among the greatest and most skilful competitors in the English game. Paul McGrath stood toe-to-toe with all-comers in the top flight and was a wonderful servant to both his clubs and country.*

STEPHEN O'FLYNN *Stephen O'Flynn is a well-known and respected player in Irish domestic football, but gives a detailed account of the rigours of trying to break into the first team at a Premier League club.*

RONNIE WHELAN *The great Ronnie Whelan left Home Farm for Liverpool in 1979 and accumulated 13 major honours in a glorious spell at Anfield. Whether we will ever see another Irishman repeat his feats seems hugely unlikely.*

perception of the game became muddied, with internal club politics and the sight of fellow young players getting ahead of themselves starting to wear thin.

'The attitude of players and managers was the main reason for my decision,' Supple told me.

'Some players are more interested in the big house, money, cars. It's not how I see things,' he says.

Doubts, he admits, had crept into his head not long after his Ipswich debut but he stuck with it, initially fearing that he would disappoint too many people if he walked away.

When Joe Royle departed as the manager in 2006, Shane also almost quit. Royle had championed Supple's cause and the keeper was dismayed at his departure.

Again he stuck with it, but it eventually became too much to take. Shane couldn't pretend any more and approached Roy Keane to express a desire to quit. Three days later, he sold his house in England, and moved back to Dublin.

Supple suggested that he might have enjoyed football more as a professional 30 years ago and he was complimentary about Ipswich, where he enjoyed living.

But ultimately, a lengthy career in the game didn't appeal.

'People couldn't get their heads around it but I wasn't happy in my life, it was as simple as that,' says Supple.

Once home, Supple re-entered education and rejoined his local Gaelic football club. He imagined following his father Brendan into the police force, but has since worked as the head of football at Legacy Sports and Entertainment Consultants, which sees him involved in the management of young Irish players, as well as scouting new talent from both Ireland and overseas. And in 2016, he returned to competitive football in the League of Ireland.

In my eyes, Supple showed immense bravery to reach his life-changing decision. He could have easily – like many of us – ambled through the rest of his career without enjoyment. He could have become extremely wealthy through football but he decided to discard all that and instead stick staunchly to his principles and personality.

He tried football as a career for several years, and was pretty good at it. But ultimately, what he saw on the inside was opposed to his personality. His decision showed conviction and when he expressed concern that some of his Ipswich team-mates were not bothered about winning or losing, it becomes clear how such negativity might play with the mind of a previously enthusiastic 18-year-old.

Ross Gaynor was another player to grow disillusioned with life in England. But in his case, it was the shifting sands of management that led to his decision to leave.

Having signed for Millwall at the age of 15, from Belvedere in Dublin, Gaynor steadily progressed through the Millwall system, helped by a loan spell with non-league Sutton United in 2007. His ascent to professional football had been rapid, as Gaynor only started playing the game aged 13. His first love had been Gaelic football and he dreamed of representing his native County Louth, not Man United or Liverpool.

Before long though, he finished as the top goalscorer in the prestigious Milk Cup, a tournament held annually in Northern Ireland, where he had played for the Dundalk Schoolboy League.

'That's when the interest started from England,' he says. 'I couldn't believe it. In my first trial with

Manchester City, Micah Richards knocked me unconscious in a practice match! The trials were a real wake-up call, as the kids over there were physically much stronger,' he says.

'Millwall came into the picture soon after and I really liked it there. They were usually around mid-table in the Championship and I would get more chances there compared to Manchester City, who had made strong efforts to get me back,' he adds.

The Scotsman Mark McGhee was the Millwall manager when Gaynor signed, but the former Aberdeen and Celtic star was soon dismissed. Former Chelsea hero Dennis Wise took over and steered Millwall to the FA Cup Final.

'Dennis liked me and two weeks after my 17th birthday drafted me into the first-team squad. I made the bench a few times and that's when I first saw the ridiculous money involved in playing senior football. Making the bench was worth three times the usual scholarship wage. But when Dennis left, in 2005, it went downhill for me,' says Ross.

A spate of managers would then occupy the Millwall hot-seat including Steve Claridge, Colin Lee, Dave Tuttle, Willie Donachie and Nigel Spackman.

'Spackman, in particular, didn't want young players in the team,' Gaynor says. 'He shipped me out on loan to Sutton but in hindsight he probably did me a favour, as it improved my game'.

Eventually, Gaynor would leave Millwall when Kenny Jackett took the reins.

'Jackett actually gave me my first start for Millwall and I made six or seven first-team appearances. But when he offered only a six-month contract for the 2007/08 season,

I was very unhappy. I had a couple of offers in England but decided that my life needed to change. I could have stayed to be a bit-part player or dropped into League 2 or the non-league, but I wasn't happy doing that. I wanted a different challenge and to be happy in myself, so coming back to Ireland seemed the only way to achieve that. I knew the manager at Cobh Ramblers, who were in the League of Ireland Premier Division, and agreed to sign a six-month contract,' he explains.

Despite falling out of love with English football, Gaynor would never discourage anyone from trying their luck there.

'It was a brilliant experience. I stayed with three young players, in digs with an elderly couple. They treated us like their own sons. We eventually got an apartment near Bromley when we turned 18. Living in London was surreal, for me. It was so busy the whole time, a bit different than Ardee! I couldn't criticise Millwall or their supporters. The fans get a hard time and they're a difficult group to have against you. They make life hard for visiting teams but it's because they love Millwall so much. Ask anyone that has played for Millwall and they will tell you the support is unbelievable,' says Ross.

Gaynor was an attacker in his younger days but has since converted to left-back, a position from which he helped Sligo Rovers (one of the few Irish clubs that offer full-time professional contracts) to win the League of Ireland in 2012. He also won the FAI Cup the following year. Aside from Sligo and Cobh, Gaynor has played for the two Louth clubs, Dundalk and Drogheda, and joined Cork City in 2014 before a spell in Northern Ireland.

A former team-mate of Gaynor at Sligo, Dublin-born defender Gavin Peers, also made a premature exit from the English game, making his decision to depart having been pushed to the fringes (at two clubs) by a change in manager. Peers had signed for Blackburn Rovers in 2003, in favour of moving to Aston Villa, where he had undergone successful trials training and playing with Gabby Agbonlahor, Gary Cahill and Luke Moore (all future first-team players for Villa).

Then a sturdy right-back, Peers signed a two-year scholarship contract, eight years after Blackburn had won the Premier League. This gave Peers two years to impress enough to earn a full-time professional contract with Blackburn.

Graeme Souness, the former Liverpool midfielder, was the manager and having learned quickly in the Under-17s, Peers was quickly catapulted into the Under-19 and reserve teams.

'I was physically strong, so that wasn't a problem, but all of a sudden I was pitched in with Steven Reid and Craig Short, Paul Dickov and Dwight Yorke, who had all played for the reserves from time to time. My reserve debut was against Manchester United and they had Eric Djemba-Djemba, Kleberson and Kieran Richardson. Souness brought me into the squad for pre-season and I was going to play in the League Cup when he [Souness] departed for Newcastle United. That was a big blow for me and life at Blackburn was never the same. It showed that, in football, you can be on the verge of great things but have it swept from under your feet by one decision or by one managerial move. Mark Hughes came in and had no time for me. He put me back in the Under-19s. I was never going to get a chance with him and he made that pretty clear, so when my agent said that Mansfield Town wanted me, I decided to go there for six months.'

Roddy Collins, who would later manage in England, had been managing Shamrock Rovers and he tried to tempt Peers into returning to Dublin.

'I wasn't ready to come home and wanted to succeed in England. In fairness to Roddy, he recommended me to the Mansfield manager, Carlton Palmer. I scored on my Mansfield debut and was flying, leading a few Championship clubs to monitor my progress. But when Carlton Palmer resigned and Peter Shirtliff came in, I wasn't part of the plans,' Gavin says.

'In Shirtliff's early days, I scored against Stockport, around Christmas 2006, and had made around 30 appearances in the season. But a few days after Stockport, I was brought to an away game and left sitting in the stand. I phoned my parents to tell them that I'd had enough and to come over to pick me up. I didn't want to think about football, I was turned off it completely.'

Peers, it seems, was definitely unlucky in England. For your career to be altered by managerial change would seem to be fairly routine, as different managers have different ideas on the game. They seek a certain type of player to carry out their playing philosophy.

But for that to happen twice, in quick succession, is fairly soul-destroying. His story taught me about the narrow margins that exist between 'making it' in England or otherwise.

It seems that a player's on-field quality, character and potential are taken into consideration when decisions are made about their future. But it also seems that big decisions often boil down to the simple whims of an individual, usually the manager.

For example, I spoke to an Irish player who moved to an English second tier club over ten years ago. He initially blossomed but eventually fell out with the manager. The player was forced to move to pastures new, in the process dropping down a division, where he found happiness at his new club until a new manager came in. Unfortunately for the player in question, the new manager had been a personal friend of his former boss (the one he had fallen out with). Cruelly, the player was immediately told that he was surplus to requirements, without even having a single training session in which to impress the new manager.

Despite its global nature, football in England remains a close-knit community, where managers talk, and maybe even gossip a little, about players. And rightly or wrongly, opinions can be formed on hearsay or whether a certain player has fallen out with other managers or coaches. This makes football no different to other forms of employment but it can occasionally make a footballer's life very difficult.

Peers, thankfully, eventually rediscovered his passion for the game, signing for Sligo Rovers and becoming a respected centre-back. He never really felt like 'a failure' after England. He was more dismayed and discouraged by how certain managers can dictate, to an extent, a footballer's future life.

For the former Nottingham Forest trainee, Brian Cash, from Portmarnock in Dublin, 'failure' was a word he couldn't get out of his head after struggling to make the grade in England.

Indeed, during our interview for this book, it was saddening to hear Cash use the word 'failure' on more than one occasion when, in my opinion, Cash – and the many young Irish players released by English clubs – have absolutely nothing to feel ashamed of. On the contrary, I suggest they should feel great pride for sampling English football for two or three years, an accomplishment that is out of reach for the vast majority of aspiring Irish footballers.

Everybody has differing views of what success and failure mean. For some people, getting out of bed is an achievement in itself. Some are happy to get through the day. Others need to climb a mountain or run a certain number of kilometres to feel good. The gauge of 'success' differs from case to case and the only real difference, for footballers, is that their 'failures' are watched and analysed by thousands of people. When your pride is battered and you feel embarrassed for not reaching other people's expectations, whether they are fair or not, that's when the mind can take you to negative places.

In the case of many young footballers, 'failure', it seems, is the price that they pay for early success; for outshining their underage peers. Cash, for example, was a revelation in underage football for Portmarnock and Home Farm and then in the Irish underage sides. He signed for Nottingham Forest, aged 15, and did enough in the next two years to warrant a three-year professional contract.

Looking back on happier times, he says: 'The Forest coaches could not have treated me or the other Irish boys any better. They looked after every aspect of our lives.'

He was never bothered by homesickness, as the club's Irish contingent was strong with goalkeeper Barry

Roche, Niall McNamara and Andy Reid (a future Ireland international) all playing for the club.

The quartet would play together for club and country, and dreamed of breaking into the first team together. But as time wore on, Cash would make just a handful of appearances in the first team and was loaned to Swansea City, then toiling in the lower leagues, and to Rochdale, who were labouring even further behind.

Slowly, Cash could see his dream fading but he felt powerless to halt the decline.

'Mainly, I was stuck in the reserves. I wasn't getting on well and was stuck in a rut. I lost my confidence, as well, because I felt I was falling short,' he says.

Cash would remain a Forest player for five years but after the loan moves, in particular, he felt unwanted.

'Leaving Forest was probably coming for a while,' he reflects.

'Eventually, the club wanted me off the wage bill and they paid the final six months of my contract. My agent assisted me in this period but Forest didn't. This period and some of the other experiences I had in England taught me that the only way to get by, in football, is to be totally selfish,' he says.

Cash joined Bristol Rovers on non-contract terms but only played in one game before moving back to Ireland with Derry City. From there, he transferred to Sligo.

'It was almost impossible to readjust to playing in Ireland,' Brian says.

'The way I saw it was that I had failed [in England]. I didn't achieve what I set out to do, to achieve the dream I'd had since I was a kid. I had big problems with confidence for a couple of years [after England]. My career in Ireland was pretty average for my ability. At Derry, I struggled with confidence and the style of play. Sligo was slightly better – considering I missed a year through injury – and generally, I had two and a half happy years there,' he says.

Cash would later play for St Patrick's Athletic and Galway but retired after leaving the latter in 2011. He runs a gymnasium and personal training studio in Dublin and believes he could, one day, work in football again as a strength and conditioning coach.

These players had a lot to offer English football but they returned home, potential unfulfilled, for varying reasons.

For Cash, Gaynor and Yadolahi, there was a reluctance to continue their careers in England's lesser divisions. But there are many Irish players content with life in the lower leagues, where they battle away and make an honest wage in less than heralded circumstances. It certainly is not fashionable and the bright lights of the Premier League are a million miles away. But it's this strand of the game and the Irish in it that we look at in the next chapter.

Chapter 5

Underneath
the Stars

NOT every young football player can be the next David Beckham, Ryan Giggs or Roy Keane. In fact, the majority of young players in England's academy system never come close to achieving the sporting and financial fortunes of these superstars.

For many, the decision by clubs to terminate their association with young players on completion of their academy scholarships is the end of the dream. It is painfully final and many never recover from the blow.

In a number of cases once promising young players simply fall out of love with the game. Dejected, they drift away from the sport they used to adore. The stigma of being rejected and failing to meet the expectations of academy coaches, and in some cases those of family and friends, is a heavy cross to bear.

And sadly, that burden can get hold of some players and they turn to other vices like alcohol, drugs and gambling to ease the pain and sense of utter rejection. With no more football in their lives and substandard education – having mostly gone overseas in their mid-teens – they are lost to the game and facing the rest of their lives riddled with self-doubt and lack of confidence and self-esteem. In extreme cases they can find it difficult to ever get back on track. It is one of the saddest aspects of football.

Yet, there is hope and other alternatives for young players who could not make the grade at the highest level. And with a little positivity, guidance and good fortune, players can recover from these major personal and professional setbacks.

For while players incapable of readjusting their once lofty ambitions drift aimlessly out of the game, many others are retuning career goals and getting on with the task of staying in professional football outside the glare of the Premier League. While not unambitious people, these characters are just mentally better than most in accepting the fact that it is hugely difficult to have long-term careers in the top flight. Their strength of character somehow enables them to keep going and to prove to people that they are good enough, and strong-willed enough, to be professional footballers. And if that means playing an entire career in League 1 or League 2 then so be it. They will never be millionaires – but still have more glamorous lives than most, make quite decent money and enjoy the prestige of being a professional footballer. Okay, it might not be how they once envisaged the dream. But it's a whole lot better than disappearing from the game altogether.

These players are heroic in their own way – because they continue fighting for the dream despite the setbacks and naysayers and manage to find the desire to soldier on manfully at a less renowned and less glamorous level.

Mark Connolly, for example, looked to have the world at his feet when, as a promising 17-year-old defender in 2009, he was transferred from Wolverhampton Wanderers to Premier League Bolton Wanderers for £1m. From Monaghan, Connolly had already captained the Wolves youth team and played in the reserves. He had never felt like moving on from Wolves, where former Ireland captain Mick McCarthy was the manager. McCarthy, says Connolly, had taken great interest in Connolly's development and been an inspiration, in many ways.

But when the director of the Wolves Academy, Chris Evans, left to join Bolton (as assistant manager to Gary Megson), he wanted to take Connolly with him. And according to Connolly, it was Evans who really forced the deal through, despite the reluctance of Wolves to allow one of its best assets to leave. Evans persisted though, says Connolly, and did everything in his power to convince Megson that parting with £1m to acquire Connolly would be fantastic business.

Even still, Connolly was unsure about moving. He felt somewhat attached to Wolves, the club who gave him an opportunity in English football.

'At first, I hesitated about moving,' says Connolly.

'I was a young boy from a close-knit community in Monaghan and never thought, for a second, that I could be worth anything like £1m. Wolves were unhappy over the approach but Chris [Evans] was just doing his new job for Bolton. I had captained the youth team for Wolves and played in the reserves at 16, so I was on the way up there. But Bolton persisted and was an established Premier League club, so I was flattered by the interest.'

The move eventually happened but Connolly was never the same player, he admits.

'To be honest, the transfer fee was a large burden. Every interview I did was about the fee. People always wanted to know about being a million-pound teenager and it was all a bit much. It added extra pressure that I didn't need in that stage of my development. I should have been enjoying football. But my life changed dramatically. I was out on my own, not knowing how to cook or clean, and it was a huge shock to the system,' he says.

During our interview, the affable and grounded Connolly almost seemed embarrassed by the transfer fee paid by Bolton.

After all, Connolly is just an Irish country boy who once jetted home (without permission from Wolves) to play for his county in an Ulster Gaelic Football Minor Championship Final, which Monaghan lost against Tyrone.

He is also a person who goes out of his way seeking new Irish players in England; to have a chat and see if he can assist them in settling in England.

But despite captaining Bolton's reserves and earning a place in the first-team squad for a League Cup match in 2011, Connolly soon became a peripheral figure at Bolton, especially when Megson left and was replaced by the once-capped Ireland international, Owen Coyle. He spent time on loan with St Johnstone in Scotland and then at lowly Macclesfield Town. But he couldn't force his way into Coyle's thoughts. Among those standing in his way was the current England defender Gary Cahill and a string of players, like Zat Knight and David Wheater, who were familiar with top-flight football.

'It was unfortunate when Megson left and after that everything changed. I was never going to convince Coyle that I could do the job in the first team. In fairness to Bolton they agreed not to ask for a transfer fee if a club became interested. But it was disheartening the way it didn't work out. There was some interest from Crystal Palace, but in the end I settled on a two-year contract with Crawley and that's where I rediscovered my love for the game,' he recalls.

In 2013, Connolly was out of contract after two years with Crawley and joined Kilmarnock in the Scottish Premier League. He has since returned for another stint at Crawley. And thankfully, his outlook on the game has changed since the dark days at Bolton.

'I probably wouldn't have been able to do this kind of interview a couple of years ago because my head was all over the place after Bolton. It was hard to understand how it could go so wrong in such a short period of time. Back then it felt like everything was against me. Some people, looking from the outside, regard you as a failure for getting released and they doubt your ability. But I know, for a fact, that many club decisions are not entirely football related. The wage bill is taken into consideration and that's fair enough; football is big business now. But it would be good if people understood this and didn't categorise released players as failures. It's important for young players to keep going in their career, even if they're released by Premier League clubs. They need to realise that the Premier League, while a wonderful place to earn a living, is not everything. They have to find ways to enjoy their football, which is what I managed, and remember that there are more important things in life, like family,' Connolly says.

For Connolly, proving his doubters wrong was one thing. But more importantly, in the years since leaving Bolton and the Premier League, he has proved to himself that he has the ability and strength of character to bounce back from setbacks.

Indeed, character and perseverance are all-important for young players, especially when, like Colin Larkin, they are faced with a major choice; either to soldier on in the lower leagues or to head home to Dundalk when it became clear that he wouldn't continue as a player for Wolves.

Back in 1999, Larkin sprang from the substitutes' bench, aged 17, to score on his Wolves debut in the League Cup against Wycombe Wanderers.

'I still remember my debut to this day and it still ranks as one of my favourite memories. I was just 17 and got thrown in for the last 20 minutes and to make it even better I scored after about five minutes; a volley at the back post. It was a special moment and I actually ended up celebrating with Darren Bazeley, an established first-teamer whose boots I was cleaning at the time,' Larkin fondly recalls.

Back then it was commonplace for trainees and young professionals to have certain daily chores to carry out in and around the club including cleaning the boots of first-team players.

'As youth players we were usually in for 9am to make sure all the jobs were done; cleaning the boots, pumping up the balls and counting and bagging them, cleaning the first-team dressing room, the referee's room, and laying out all the training kits for the professionals. We even had to have several pots of tea ready for them. Then we helped carry the goals to the training pitch before starting our own training session. After training, if the first team weren't finished, we waited until the end to put the goals away. Then you made sure that all the senior players' boots were cleaned and we went over all the previously mentioned jobs again. I remember in my first few weeks of full-time training almost falling asleep on the bus on the way home. We trained four days a week and went to college every Thursday, where I did a two-year business management course. We played a match every Saturday morning and then reported to the ground for whatever duties needed to be done. I know academy players nowadays have it easier. For instance, they don't have the jobs we had and don't even clean the boots. In my case those jobs helped mould me. And it built teamwork because everyone was punished if everything wasn't done. But I loved it and breaking into the Wolves team was brilliant,' says Larkin.

But for Larkin, making a long-term impression for Wolves was extremely difficult. He made only three appearances in three seasons, and he knew that his future was up in the air.

'I always think back to when I left Wolves, and every time it comes in my head I know I made the right decision,' he says.

'Okay, for some players it would be very difficult to leave clubs like Wolves. It's a very big club with huge history and I had two years remaining on my contract. But when I looked at my situation, it was clear that

Wolves were moving on without me. They were very keen to get into the Premier League and were signing great players like Paul Ince and Denis Irwin. I needed regular first-team football and it wasn't going to happen at Wolves. I left the club in 2002 but the real catalyst for moving was a loan move to Kidderminster Harriers in the previous year. Having played well at Kidderminster I knew that I needed to get out of Wolves, and to just play every week. I didn't want to waste more time sitting on the bench and in the stands. I made a lot of sacrifices to be a professional player and wasn't happy to just be a squad player,' he adds.

And so, Larkin's journey through the lower leagues began. Even though Jan Molby, who had taken him on loan to Kidderminster, wanted to sign him for Hull City, Larkin eventually joined Mansfield Town, who had been promoted to the third tier.

'People ask how you can drop down the divisions. But I felt it was stepping up. Of course I wonder what might have happened if I'd stayed at Wolves. But everything happens for a reason, in my opinion, and I suppose my life wouldn't have turned out the way it has if I hadn't moved. Sometimes you've got to make hard decisions and I am happy with the way it turned out,' says Colin, who later refused a move back to hometown club Dundalk to continue his career in England. By then, he had played for Chesterfield, Hartlepool United, Lincoln City and Northampton Town.

'Yeah, the opportunity came because Ian Foster, my former team-mate at Kidderminster, was managing Dundalk. It might have been a good thing but I knew I had more to give in English football. I was playing quite well for Hartlepool and I had settled in England with my family. Dundalk was the only Irish team I would've considered signing for but when you play in England, and in professional football, it's probably difficult to let it go. I wanted to keep going, to keep battling and playing as high in the league as possible,' he says.

In 2013, Larkin dropped into the non-league ranks in England, where he has played for Harrogate Town, Gateshead, West Auckland Town and Sunderland RCA. He has no regrets about his career and encourages players who are released by big clubs to continue having faith in their ability.

'You go to England, in the first place, because you're a good player. I didn't have the likes of Manchester United scouting me for nothing; I could play a bit. And it's the same for every player who goes to England. They should never forget that they have good ability and that you can keep going even when you suffer disappointment,' Colin says.

David Mooney is another Irishman with a tale or two about rejection and disappointment in England.

For having scored a bagful of goals in the League of Ireland for Shamrock Rovers, Longford Town and Cork City, Mooney moved to Reading for £250,000 in 2008.

But for three years on from signing, Mooney was simply pushed aside; ignored by various managers and shifted from pillar to post in a spate of loan moves that offered respite from his Reading nightmare but little long-term security.

'Five or six English clubs wanted to sign me but I chose Reading for its strong Irish connections and because they seemed confident in my ability,' he recalls.

'The papers claimed that I was the direct replacement for Dave Kitson, who was a great player for Reading. It looked good and I was ready to make a mark. But the manager [Steve Coppell] simply didn't play me. Coppell did great things for Reading but for me, he promised a lot and never delivered. I never got a chance and it was mentally draining. I was pushed to the side, as players are when not in the team. I was on the verge of an international call-up when I joined Reading but suddenly found myself in the abyss,' he says.

That he was overlooked by Coppell had come as a surprise to Mooney, especially as the Berkshire club had such a strong association with Irish players.

They had signed Kevin Doyle and Shane Long, both from Cork City, and given them plenty of first-team exposure. The Hunt brothers, Noel and Stephen, also featured prominently for Reading. The club knew the Irish market well and had benefited greatly from various purchases from the League of Ireland. They knew that there was value in signing Irish players for relatively small amounts and turning them into excellent performers in the Premier League. Then, they could sell the players on for hefty profits. In Kevin Doyle's case, Reading paid Cork City around £78,000 for his signature. And three years later he joined Wolves for £6.6m. Reading also received over £6m when selling Shane Long to West Bromwich Albion in 2011.

For many, it seems preposterous that clubs pursue players and spend a good amount of time and money assessing them only to leave the said players languishing in the reserves. But that's exactly what happened to Mooney.

'Look, football is not all doom and gloom and has its good moments. But you need to work really hard to succeed and be prepared for getting through some hard times to reach better days. Honestly, after what I've seen in English football I wouldn't encourage my own son to be a footballer. It can be such a cruel industry. I was full of beans when I signed for Reading, ready to make a big impact and eyeing an international call-up but it quickly unravelled. Being on the end of rejection after rejection, which happened at Reading, really knocked me for six and I suppose you have to have thick skin for it. I sometimes wonder how I stuck it out and would warn any Irish kids going to England to be prepared for the put-downs and the knock-backs. It took me a long time to come to terms with what happened at Reading and to eventually realise my entire career didn't have to revolve around Reading. I had gone to England to be a professional footballer and I was going to achieve it with or without Reading. I could have gone home; just packed my bags and fled. But I had a desire to succeed and to stick it out,' he says.

There would have been no shortage of options for Mooney had he ditched the English adventure and a spate of League of Ireland clubs were watching the situation in case his signature became available. Moving home though would have been an easy option, he says, and he wanted to prove that he could translate his scoring prowess to the English leagues.

'When my wife and young child came over I thought that everything was falling in place,' he remembers.

'I was a professional footballer and had my family around me, too. But it became a stressful time for us when I wasn't in the team. The way that I was ruthlessly pushed aside, completely out of the picture at the club, meant that I became difficult to be around. It wasn't an enjoyable period for the people close to me, so I eventually decided that I needed to escape from Reading,' he adds.

To do so, he took a path well worn by Irish fringe players and joined third-tier Stockport County on loan. But having enjoyed the first two games for the Hatters, Mooney got injured and was forced to return to his parent club.

In March 2009, he was shipped out on loan again to Norwich City, who were embroiled in a relegation battle in the Championship (second tier).

Norwich would prove to be a breath of fresh air for Mooney. In Bryan Gunn, he found a manager who believed in his ability, and he contributed three goals in nine appearances as the Canaries eventually succumbed to the drop.

David says he regrets not trying harder to force a permanent transfer to Norwich but his cause wasn't helped as Gunn was relieved of his managerial duties. The loan spell, however, helped Mooney to rekindle the confidence garnered during a prolific League of Ireland career. And in October 2009 – with his situation unchanged at Reading – he was given another chance to impress on loan with Charlton Athletic.

Like Norwich, Charlton had recent previous in the Premier League. But they had plummeted to the third tier by 2009. They were managed by Phil Parkinson, a former Reading stalwart, who was very familiar with Mooney's strengths and weaknesses.

A knee injury early in the loan ruled Mooney out for a month. But when he returned to action he scored six goals and helped the Addicks reach the end-of-season promotion play-offs.

Unfortunately, they were beaten by Swindon Town in the play-off final at Wembley. And if the defeat wasn't hard enough to take, David was dreading returning to Reading for the start of pre-season training.

By then Coppell was no longer in charge having been replaced by the future Celtic and Liverpool manager, Brendan Rodgers.

But Mooney didn't want to be there and worse still, knew that Reading wanted shot of him, too.

Rodgers didn't last long as the manager and was replaced by Brian McDermott but no amount of managerial upheaval seemed to make any difference to Mooney's plight.

'It wasn't going to change no matter who was in charge,' he admits.

'I was 100 per cent finished as a Reading player. I trained myself to not get my hopes up regardless of managerial change. I was just trampled on so many times that I couldn't go through it any more. When nobody came in to buy me, the only thing I could do, for the 2010/11 season, was to get another loan.'

He did just that and top-scored for Colchester United, where the manager, John Ward, was a keen fan of Mooney's playing style.

As it turned out, Colchester was the ideal shop window for Mooney and when his Reading contract finally expired in the summer of 2011, several league clubs were interested in his signature.

He eventually settled for a move to Leyton Orient and his goalscoring form in the 2013/14 season led them to the play-off final. Again, however, Mooney was on the losing side at Wembley.

'The beauty of the loans, particularly with relatively big clubs like Charlton and Norwich, was that they opened my eyes to what I could achieve in England. Ideally, I wouldn't have dropped down a division to get regular football but signing for Leyton Orient was the best move I ever made. My experiences had taught me a lot about the cruelty of football. But they also taught me about sticking to the task and getting the head down and working hard when things go against you. Coming through the rough patches really helped to sustain a long-term career. I am proud of what I have achieved in England [Mooney transferred to Southend United in 2015], especially with Leyton Orient, and I think I would've regretted it had I gone home prematurely. You know, not knowing how it could have turned out; I think that would have eaten away at me,' Mooney says.

The striker is not the only player who had to readjust his ambitions in England. For although far less glamorous than the Premier League, England's lower leagues (Championship, League 1 and League 2) are now stacked full of Irish players.

For example, between the 2009/10 and 2014/15 seasons, a total of 51 Irish players have featured in the end-of-season divisional play-off finals across the three lower leagues. And in the 2015 English Championship (second tier) play-offs, eight Irish players and the former Ireland manager Mick McCarthy were involved.

Indeed, if you pick up any newspaper after a round of weekend matches in England you will quickly see that the Irish players making an impact in England are doing so well below the Premier League. On any given weekend there can be up to 20 Irish players turning out for League 2 clubs and in most cases their English careers started with teams higher up the league structure.

Some of these players are forced to become journeyman players, representing a variety of teams as they endeavour to forge the best career possible.

Jamie Devitt, for example, started his English career with Hull City. But failing to make the grade there, he settled for a raft of loan moves – with Darlington, Shrewsbury Town, Grimsby Town (twice), Bradford City, Accrington Stanley and Rotherham United – until signing permanent terms at Chesterfield and then playing for Morecambe and Carlisle United. It has been a roundabout way of maintaining his professional career. But there are huge numbers of players in the same boat.

The left-back Enda Stevens looked to be heading for big things when signing for then Premier League side Aston Villa from Shamrock Rovers in 2012. Yet, after only seven senior league games, Stevens was on his way, starting with loan moves to Notts County, Doncaster Rovers (twice) and Northampton Town and ending with a permanent transfer to Portsmouth, who had dropped to the fourth tier despite winning the FA Cup Final as recently as 2008. Stevens was joined in the Portsmouth squad by the veteran Irish forward Noel Hunt, who was mentioned earlier in this chapter for playing for Reading. More recently, he dropped into the lower leagues to play for Southend United and Portsmouth.

Other Irish players to become established and respected lower league performers include the defender Alan Sheehan, winger Graham Carey and goalkeeper

Barry Roche. And they are surrounded in the league's lower reaches by fellow countrymen like former League of Ireland players Jake Carroll and Kevin Dawson.

For many of these players there must have been moments when self-doubt crept in. Am I actually good enough for professional football? Should I just cut my losses and return home? Where on earth is my career actually going? And do I genuinely want to be hopping from club to club, almost annually, just to earn a living? Is all the training and personal sacrifice worth it? These are all valid questions that lower league footballers can ask themselves. But what keeps many going is not the thought of potential greater wealth and the recognition that playing for bigger clubs can bring. Instead, says the diminutive Carlow-born striker Padraig Amond, a sheer undying love for the sport is what motivates.

'I have had a great time in English football and if clubs continue wanting me then I could easily stay another ten years,' says Amond, who first appeared in English football in 2011 for Accrington Stanley.

'I feel very lucky to have the chance to be a professional and really enjoy it. It's a tough business and playing in League 2, where I've mainly played, is not for the faint-hearted. But we train as hard as any team in the country, be it Rochdale or Manchester United, and are looked after well by our clubs. It's a pressurised job because you're always expected to win. But that's part of it and we, as footballers, get paid quite well, so we can't complain too much,' says Padraig, who has also played in Portugal's top division for Pacos de Ferreira.

But what kind of money can lower league players earn? Well, compared to the astronomical figures being paid in the Premier League, it sort of dwarfs into insignificance. Yet, to the ordinary worker, lower league players are still dealing with very reasonable amounts.

Of course, it comes nowhere near the Premier League average weekly wage, which by 2014 was just under £44,000, giving top-flight English footballers the highest average wages in world football – 60 per cent higher than the second highest earning league, the Bundesliga in Germany.

Lower league wages are even far removed from the average pay in the Championship (England's second tier), where players receive an average weekly wage of about £5,000. The top players in the Championship can earn up to £10,000 a week while the average weekly wage in League 1 is between £1,700 and £2,500. That figure drops to between £1,300 and £1,500 in League 2, potentially taking annual earnings for a top League 2 player to about £80,000 (the average annual English worker's wage was £26,500 in 2014).

Unlike in the top flight, where players sign three- and four-year contracts, the length of contracts in the bottom tiers is for far less time and usually for a year, ensuring that little long-term job security is available to players, who are often eyeing their potential next move within a few months of signing for a new club.

Still, Amond describes being a footballer as the dream job and his enthusiasm for the game is definitely infectious, particularly when you consider the harsh environment in which he operates.

His former clubs Accrington Stanley and Morecambe, for example, generally struggle to stay afloat in the Football League and often attract, shall we say, a more seasoned and hardened type of professional; the worldly-wise and more cynical, robust players. These players, usually in their mid-30s, can be well journeyed and the only count that matches their total number of previous clubs is the number of scars on their bodies; the physical evidence of a lifetime spent scrapping in the backwaters of the professional game.

These players have fought the good fight for many years, when others might have given up. And they have admirably battled to make enough money to keep their families going.

But the battle to stay afloat in the game can slowly eat away at the once innocent love of football. And taking the place of past affection for the sport is a single-minded, individual approach to what is, fundamentally, the mother of all team games. They do whatever it takes to stay in the team and earn enough money to remain financially stable. If they reach the end of the road at one club, it doesn't really matter where the next contract comes from. The main thing is merely getting a reasonable contract, no matter where or how, and it doesn't concern them whether it's with minnows like Accrington and Morecambe, who both average fewer than 2,000 supporters for home games.

These players walk over anybody who gets in the way and the further down the leagues you go, the more hard-hitting and brutal it becomes, which means that strikers, like Amond, are regularly pitted against physically superior centre-backs, who use any means of getting the ball ahead of the man. They don't take prisoners and do what they have to. Nippy strikers, like Padraig, have to be braced for the next big hit and always be on their toes – if a six-foot-plus defender is not already standing on them!

None of this, however, seems to faze Amond, who remains boyishly enamoured by the English game. Refreshingly, he says that the sporting element of being a professional and representing a close-knit, community-based club outweighs the relevance of his bank account. At writing, Amond had moved back into the Football League with Hartlepool United after a spell in the non-league.

His story, like all those in this chapter, is not about making millions of pounds and starring on *Match of the Day* every week. The magazines and newspapers don't follow you around and not everybody knows your name. But his story is one of perseverance and resilience and offers tremendous hope to young players devastated by the shock of not making it at the very highest level. You see, if you really love the game and stoically persist with your dream, your sporting and personal life can be just as fulfilling, even if the bank balance and sense of recognition is not as great as your Premier League peers.

Chapter 6

Kerr-Plunk and the Dokter's Medicine

TO find a long-term cure for the ills in Ireland's youth set-up, the Football Association of Ireland (FAI) turned to a Dutchman in 2013.

Ruud Dokter, a generally media-shy unknown quantity in Ireland before his appointment as association high performance director, was charged with the task of overseeing the non-senior international men's programme, the women's senior and underage international programmes, and coach education and player development.

Then aged 57, Dokter came to Ireland with an unremarkable playing career behind him and instead, boasted an admirable background in developing young players in his homeland and in Qatar.

Given Dutch football's reputation for developing young players blessed with sublime technique, and for churning out really good coaches, it was probably no surprise that the FAI continued its fascination with that country's coaches when Dokter's predecessor, his fellow Dutchman Wim Koevermans, had departed the role.

Now, there has never been any doubting the Dutch system for producing fine footballers. It has worked for many years and will continue to do so. And Dokter, of course, does have the necessary qualifications and knowledge to carry out the role. Indeed, his agreeing to a new four-year contract extension in 2016 suggests that the FAI think there's nobody capable of doing a better job.

But despite Dokter's background, steeped as it is in player development, was it actually necessary for the FAI to look outside its own country when considering a replacement for Koevermans?

For in the same year in which Dokter took residence in Dublin, arguably the city's most respected and cunning youth coach ever was boarding a ship for one of Europe's most obscure football outposts, the Faroe Islands, to resurrect an illustrious coaching career somewhat tainted by his dismissal, by the FAI, as Ireland senior team manager in 2005.

For Brian Kerr, a man simply unrivalled for his insight on all strands of Irish football, was surely the right person for the high performance role. He had already filled the position as association technical director and had been a revelation as Ireland's most successful underage coach. But instead of being given the keys to the future of the game in his own country, Kerr was forced to turn to coaching the Faroes, a genuine minnow of world football, and that seemed a downright pity, and very much an oversight on behalf of the FAI.

Kerr had been successful in League of Ireland management, where he loyally served St Patrick's Athletic for a decade, winning two league titles. But his record as head coach of the various Irish underage teams was unrivalled. In 1997, he steered the Under-20 team to a third-place finish at the FIFA Under-20 World Cup and a year later was at the helm as Ireland won the UEFA U16 and U18 European Championships.

That period represents Ireland's most successful ever at any level in the game, and was a breeding ground for future senior team stars like Damien Duff, Richard Dunne, Robbie Keane and John O'Shea.

It was also a period that helped show the world that Ireland has the capability and expertise to produce outstanding young players. And for that, Kerr and his popular and equally respected assistant, the late Noel O'Reilly, deserve huge recognition.

Their successes in European and world competitions also dispelled a notion that Irish teams, whether in football, cricket or rugby, can only make it so far without having the mentality and/or skill to see the job through to its end.

Seeing groups of young Irish players conquer the world's best teams put a spring in the step of the country's football fraternity, and it gave them the kind of confidence and self-worth that many Irish teams (and people) would struggle to boast about – both before and after the success of Kerr's young teams.

It was this same lack of belief and confidence in our own that arguably played a part in Kerr getting overlooked for the high performance job. Of course, the FAI can defend itself by saying that the ultimate trust and confidence had been put in Kerr when he was appointed national team manager in 2003.

Now, Kerr's spell as Ireland senior manager was not dynamic. Like when he managed St Patrick's Athletic, his tactics could be perceived as quite conservative, especially if his team went ahead in games, and some of his substitutions as Ireland manager were questionable, too.

Indeed, not many people forget how Kerr's team threw away hopes of qualifying for the 2006 World Cup by squandering leads against Israel, who were a decent side but nothing spectacular and a team that Ireland should really have been beating. But in the first meeting of the sides in Tel Aviv, Ireland went into their shell having taken the lead just before half-time. Ultimately, the defensive policy didn't work, as Israel grabbed a devastating equaliser through Abbas Suan's long-range drive in the last minute of normal time. Less than three months later, Ireland looked easily capable of dismissing the Israelis in Dublin having built a 2-0 lead by the 11th minute. Yet, Ireland again stood off their opponents, almost criminally allowing the visitors back in the game. When Israel scored in the 39th minute, the mind flashed back to that fateful night in Tel Aviv. And after they equalised, to earn another unlikely draw, huge question marks would hang over Kerr's approach to handling games at the top level.

As they say, to make a mistake once is perhaps understandable. But to repeat the same mistake was bordering on negligence.

Despite that, and the fact Kerr's team could only muster five points from six qualifying games against the main group rivals (France, Israel and Switzerland), Ireland were still in the race for qualification going into the final group game, at home against Switzerland. The Swiss had one point more than Ireland and knew that a draw in Dublin would secure second place in the group and a play-off to reach the World Cup. The sides had drawn in Basel earlier in the group; Ireland again throwing away an early lead to draw one apiece (though Kerr was not the manager at the time). Still, Ireland knew that a victory, in front of a partisan home crowd, would see them leapfrog the Swiss and finish a topsy-turvy campaign in second place. To give some context to the fixture, Ireland were without two of their most gifted players, Damien Duff and Roy Keane, and the Swiss were a very decent outfit capable of moments of quality. Yet, you felt that Ireland, at home, would have the battling qualities and desire to find a way through. But it never happened and the game finished scoreless. The Swiss progressed to the World Cup play-offs and Ireland had bowed out.

Afterwards, Kerr came in for some stinging criticism from former professionals/pundits and John Giles described Ireland's second half performance as shambolic and littered with aimless long balls. Ray Houghton, the hero of past tournaments for Ireland, said the country had gone out of the tournament with a whimper, while Liam Brady was perturbed by the lack of expression in Ireland's play, asking how the team could be so rigid in its approach and never try to beat their opponent with skill or trickery down the flanks.

On the other hand, Ireland had been marvellous in Paris earlier in the group, producing a stoic and quite expressive display against an outstanding French side. Somehow, Ireland could only achieve a scoreless draw in the French capital but a win had probably been merited.

Later in the group, the French would beat Ireland in Dublin.

And still, there were other positives in Kerr's tenure, as he was responsible for convincing Roy Keane, one of the last truly great Irish players, to end his premature international retirement.

To do so, Kerr was able to show great compassion to leave behind the furore caused by Keane's bust-up with the previous manager, Mick McCarthy, at the 2002 World Cup in South Korea and Japan, where Ireland performed in remarkably spirited fashion despite their captain's high-profile exit from the squad.

Indeed, they were only eliminated in the last 16 stage against a brilliant Spanish side (on penalties after a drawn match), leaving many to wonder what might have been possible had Keane, the driving force behind Ireland's qualification and Manchester United's star captain, been at the heart of the midfield.

But Kerr banished all that to the past and instead, saw Keane's absence from the Ireland squad as a national disaster. In his own down-to-earth style, Kerr carefully arranged for Keane to make a smooth return to the fold; the skipper eventually rejoining the squad for a match against Romania, in May 2004.

Indeed, Kerr handled the whole situation brilliantly. Naturally, the media furore that accompanied Keane's return was as frenzied as could be imagined. But Kerr, in an understated and almost elegant style, managed to quell the media circus that would always go hand-in-hand with Keane rejoining the panel.

Always refreshingly honest and regarded as a manager for the people in the street, Kerr never looked to receive any plaudits for twisting Keane's arm, or for convincing a notoriously strong-willed individual to give international football another try. Instead, he stayed regimentally focused on what he tried to achieve with the team, knowing that Keane's return would only serve to bolster Ireland's chances of qualifying for the 2006 World Cup. In the end, Keane's injury-enforced absence for the Swiss match, coupled with the loss of the supremely skilful Duff (for similar reasons) meant that Ireland didn't have the strength in depth to cope in their absence. In Keane's case particularly, Ireland didn't have a midfielder in the same class, meaning that utility defender John O'Shea was pressed into an auxiliary midfield role in the Swiss game. And without Duff's wing wizardry, Ireland would revert to more direct tactics, hoping (ultimately in vain) that the likes of Gary Doherty, Stephen Elliott and Clinton Morrison would conjure something up. But they never did (despite Ian Harte missing a great early chance). And Kerr would fall on his sword.

Though Kerr would pay for Ireland's faults by losing his job, his record as the Ireland manager (statistically at least) stands relatively proud compared to his predecessors. For in his 33-game tenure, Ireland lost only four times, leaving Kerr with a win percentage of 55 per cent.

Naturally, Kerr probably has regrets about his senior team tenure. But hey, name a manager who doesn't look back and have at least some regrets? For example, even the legendary Alex Ferguson, despite winning 13 Premier League titles, five FA Cup Finals, and two Champions League trophies with Manchester United, has spoken of majorly regretting the build-up to the Champions League semi-final in 2002, which United lost against Bayer

Leverkusen. And perhaps the most successful manager in the history of the Irish national team, Jack Charlton, also has regrets about how his eventful career ended with Ireland; the team being completely outclassed by Holland in the European Championships play-offs, to bring an almost inevitably downbeat end to Charlton's wonderful spell as manager.

So, Kerr was definitely not alone in that sense. When he did seem somewhat alone though, was when the huge sense of public support for his appointment began to wane, and the FAI were hardly quick to publicly back their man. In the end, there was sadness about the way they dispensed with Kerr, who for ten years had given the association invaluable service. He looked forlorn and somewhat helpless in the aftermath of the Switzerland game, which was an uncomfortable sight for people long associated with the game in Ireland. This was a good man and a very good coach, who arguably deserved much better treatment from the association and some sections of the public.

Nonetheless, championing him for the high performance role is not based on his record as senior team manager – just like his efforts as senior team manager can never dilute his record at underage level.

Instead, it just seemed so black and white. Ireland and the FAI were looking for a perfectly qualified person to revamp its underage structure and take the country forward in youth football, with a view to producing more world-class players like the international stars produced by Kerr in the 90s.

And Kerr, at the same time, was out of a job, apart from various roles in football media. Surely, his appointment would be a no-brainer? But no, he was overlooked. And perhaps, he was not even considered for the task.

For speaking to the *Irish Independent*'s Michael Verney in 2016, Kerr said he had not received any contact from the FAI since his contract as senior team manager was not renewed in 2005.

'I have had no contact,' he says.

'I have not been invited into that parlour by this Dutchman [Ruud Dokter] or the previous Dutchman [Wim Koevermans]. I think you'd have to ask them [the FAI] why that is. They were the ones who decided not to renew my contract in 2005 after I had been working for them for nearly ten years,' he adds.

Now, that scenario presents as a real pity for modern Irish football.

For how can an island of Ireland's size and population afford to overlook a person of such integrity, professionalism and standing? Nobody in the country commands the same level of respect for his achievements in football as Brian Kerr.

And even the job he achieved in the Faroe Islands, where he masterminded some rare but wonderful victories, and an unexpected draw against Northern Ireland, reflected brilliantly Kerr's ability to extract the maximum from a group of players regarded as limited in ability and potential.

There, he worked with a collection of largely part-time players (apart from four professionals in Denmark and Iceland) including builders, carpenters, fish factory workers, schoolteachers and a bowling alley employee.

Yet, the experiences garnered in the League of Ireland, where it all started for Kerr, meant he was more than able to communicate appropriately with the part-timers and to show compassion and understanding of their off-field circumstances, which sometimes could impede their ability to perform well.

He had gone from handling the demands and needs of Premier League footballers, in the Irish changing room, to valiantly trying to muster any sort of positive result with a bunch of unrecognised, unglamorous, semi-professional waifs and strays. But it didn't seem to matter to Kerr, who just wanted to coach and guide a previously derided squad to a more respectable standing in the game.

Although the scope to improve the Faroes' long-term fortunes was never too great (the local association eventually differed on the level of investment required to potentially take the islands' fortunes to the next level) he did enough to ensure the Faroes' world ranking improved slightly.

His efforts pointed to a man capable and willing to work at any level once the enjoyment was there. And in Dean Delany, Kerr's former underage goalkeeper who won the FA Youth Cup with Everton in 1998, the Dublin coach has a loyal supporter who agrees that Kerr should play a central role in the ongoing development of Irish youth football.

'Brian [Kerr] was the ideal candidate for the high performance role but it seems, to me, like the bridges were already burned [between the association and Brian; Kerr has never been shy about publicly criticising certain association policies since his dismissal as senior team manager].

'And that is a great shame, really,' says Delany, who was Kerr's goalkeeper when Ireland won the U16 and U18

European Championships and finished third at the U20 World Cup.

'He built a brilliant legacy through his work with the underage teams and in my opinion his legacy would have been enhanced further had he got the high performance job. I am sure Brian would have been a great success in the role. He has the right attributes for it. He has always been approachable and very understanding and has unbelievable knowledge of the game.

'His attention to detail was on another level and he would tell you detail after detail about players from remote countries that you had never heard of, and the information would always help you in the games. I don't think people realise the scale of his accomplishments with the underage teams.

'He just understood the mentality of young Irish players and how to get the best out of them. Look, he was an outstanding manager but what I particularly liked was the way he was interested in your life, as well as your career. He would turn up to watch you play – sometimes in meaningless matches – and would hang around after to have a chat and give analysis on how you played. He always had something positive to say and just knew what made people tick. He had an amazing way of getting to your level and inside your head, to help you as a player and a person. I think the fact Ireland's underage teams had ordinary results, since Brian left the underage section, proved what a loss he was to that strand of the game,' Delany adds.

By now, perhaps Kerr is comfortable knowing that he's unlikely to again contribute to the way in which Irish underage football is run.

But yet, if Kerr sits down to ponder the impact he could have made on the Irish football system, had he been entrusted with the high performance role, then the realisation that his days nurturing Ireland's finest young talent are (probably) over for good must be hugely frustrating for someone with so much more to give.

'I think that the people, the Irish football public, felt that Brian's promotion to the senior side, in 2003, was the natural progression for someone so successful in underage international football,' Delany recalls.

'For me, he did a great job with the senior team – given the players at his disposal. He brought a few young players into the squad, who went on to play in plenty of international matches. And I thought that his record, as the manager, was more than reasonable and that he should have been given a chance to continue in the role. His Irish team got very close to qualifying for a major tournament. But maybe the fact his teams didn't qualify, particularly for the 2006 World Cup, gave the association a chance to let him go.

'For me, he always had the support of the people but did he have the full backing of the association? Brian is very much his own man and would never be anyone's puppet. And I believe that he had ambitions to revolutionise the way Irish football was structured. Maybe he felt restrained in doing that, I don't know. I'm not privy to what went on behind the scenes but I don't think the FAI was willing to give Brian total control of the direction Irish football was headed. And maybe there was a disagreement about that, I don't know.

'Unfortunately for Brian and Irish football, and the potential young stars of tomorrow, whatever transpired seems to have dictated that he is no longer utilised by the association. And that's the greatest pity in Irish youth football at the moment,' adds Delany, who still plays the game domestically for Shelbourne.

As sad as Kerr's non-involvement is, football has a habit of moving on. Kerr has forged a respectable career in television analysis and punditry, although he has never hidden the fact that he would love to return to full-time coaching, if a suitable opportunity ever arose.

But in his absence from FAI headquarters, which since 2007 has been located at the National Sports Campus in Abbotstown, Dublin, the development of the country's grass-roots game has fallen into the hands of Ruud Dokter, whose National Player Development Plan – started in 2014 with the establishment of a Technical Advisory Group including FAI coaches Dokter and Niall Harrison, representatives from the Schoolboy Association of Ireland, FAI Schools and the SSE Airtricity League (League of Ireland) – is seen by many as holding the key to Irish football's future. In itself, the Advisory Group was a fine idea and consulted with brilliant schoolboy coaches like John Devine, a former Arsenal player and technical director of one of Dublin's most successful schoolboy leagues.

And at the very least, there finally appears to be a willingness from the FAI to change its approach to underage development. Yet, there are those who remain dubious about whether the plan will ever be carried out in its entirety. If those doubts eventually become fact, then the FAI will have a number of serious questions to answer, like why they ever even bothered hiring Dokter or indeed, Wim Koevermans? And also why they put valuable resources, time and money into researching the plan, if they were never totally committed to its proper implementation?

'There is said to be a new will about the issue and that many of the problems are starting to be addressed. That's what the FAI maintains,' says Irish football writer Miguel Delaney.

'The caveat to such a positive sense of purpose is that we have heard such plans before, we have heard what must be done for so long, but we have so far seen no real effects. The wonder, and the hope, is whether that is finally changing,' he adds.

Change, however, has rarely been flavour of the month in certain sections of a rather complex Irish underage football structure, in which parochialism and in-fighting can be commonplace.

So, one can only assume that Dokter and his associates will encounter many obstacles on the way to introducing major changes. For even when the Dutchman has spoken publicly about the plan, he usually sounds only cautiously optimistic about the future growth of the game in Ireland, which for him includes the introduction of a widespread, common philosophy to give young players more freedom on the pitch to harness creative skills.

He believes that the FAI has to begin influencing players from a younger age and that all coaches must share a common philosophy in order to create appropriate player pathways from the age of six upwards. To that end, all schoolboy leagues have been instructed to introduce U6 leagues while at the other end of the cycle Dokter has overseen the introduction of national leagues at U15, U17 and U19 levels.

Yet, according to Miguel Delaney, the greatest challenge Dokter and the FAI are facing is getting people, up and down the country, singing from the same hymn sheet.

'It is actually very difficult to describe the current shape of Irish football,' Miguel says.

'Broadly speaking, there are three main pillars: schoolboy (the SFAI), junior (the provincial FAs) and senior (the League of Ireland). Between those pillars, the links are unclear. Within them, there are even more disparate blocks and often multiple different leagues in the same county, some of them with no defined place in the structure. A kind view would call it an Escher painting. A harsh one would call it a mess.

'Rather than clear steps,' he continues, 'there have traditionally been gaps and ceilings everywhere with the situation historically complicated by endless political issues. It is for that reason that, while Dokter's end point may be clear, the path there is not. One of many catch-22s at the core of any reform is that it may require a lot of individual bodies and competitions to decide whether they must exist. Evolution is rarely painless. At the very least, Dokter's focus is clear, even if Irish football is not.'

However, other countries of similar and even lesser standing have been adequately able to put aside in-house squabbling for the greater good of their game, and to give their country's youngsters the best possible chance to develop into quality senior players.

Iceland, for example, radically overhauled its coaching and training systems in the last decade or so, eventually resulting in its senior national team qualifying for a first ever major tournament in 2016 (the European

Championships). Along the way to qualification, Iceland achieved notable victories against the Czech Republic and Holland, and the pinnacle, for a previous minnow in the game, came when they defeated England at the European Championships in France.

For many, Iceland's impact at the Championships was a massive surprise. But the transformation didn't happen overnight and was a result of sound long-term investment and innovation on the part of the Icelandic Football Association.

For although Icelandic players, like Barcelona and Chelsea star Eiður Guðjohnsen, had infiltrated Europe's best leagues for a number of years, they still had very little to boast about, domestically, as a genuine football nation.

So, they set about changing that. And in 2002, the real process of providing Iceland with long-term success started with the building of six full-size indoor football halls around the country. More than 20 artificial pitches and 130 mini-pitches were also constructed for schools and communities, enabling football to be played all year round, which given Iceland's extreme climate was not previously possible.

Admirably, they put the emphasis on training and inclusiveness and huge effort was made to improve the standard of coaching through coach development and education; a drive steered by former technical director, Sigurður Ragnar Eyjólfsson. As a result, over 70 per cent of Icelandic coaches have now gained the UEFA 'B' coaching licence, while approximately 30 per cent of domestic coaches have acquired the UEFA 'A' coaching qualifications.

Icelandic coaches focus on developing player technique between the ages of eight and twelve and the current crop of senior international players provides first-hand evidence of what can happen if a football association invests and implements a driven development plan that can transform a country's fortunes. First, the will has to be there to do it. And secondly, the finance must be put in place. But whether the FAI has either commodity is hard to say.

And if the Icelandic model is not enough to inspire change then we should look at Belgium's progress since they were eliminated at the group stage in the 1998 World Cup. Back then, the Belgians were sick and tired of falling short, both in qualification and at tournaments, and decided to completely dismantle the existing youth system and implement a brave new era.

They constructed a new national football centre on the outskirts of Brussels and the number of people enrolling on entry-level coaching courses increased ten-fold when the federation made it free of charge.

The federation joined forces with the Belgian government to introduce eight schools of sport in a four-year period (1998 to 2002) and inspired by trips to training centres in France, Holland and Germany, every youth team across the country was told to play a flexible 4-3-3 formation; the same formation favoured by the national team.

As for the success of the schools of sport, which combine education with sport and see the best train with the best, seven of Belgium's excellent 2014 World Cup squad came through the system, including regular English Premier League performers Thibaut Courtois

(Chelsea), Mousa Dembélé (Tottenham Hotspur) and Simon Mignolet (Liverpool).

Again, results didn't happen overnight. But within three years, Belgium had qualified for major international tournaments at U17 and U19 level, as the senior side quickly climbed the FIFA rankings.

From then on, as the graduates came through steadily from the schools of sport, Belgian results started to come thick and fast. And by the time they qualified for the 2014 World Cup, all but six of the squad were aged 27 or under. For a country with a population of 11 million and 34 professional clubs, their record for producing star players, in recent years, is second to none and their 2016 European Championship squad presented like a 'Who's Who' from the top English Premier League clubs including the likes of Vincent Kompany, who captained Manchester City to two league titles, and Chelsea's wonderfully gifted attacker Eden Hazard.

Belgium can also call on Premier League players Toby Alderweireld and Jan Vertonghen (Tottenham Hotspur), Marouane Fellaini (Manchester United), Thomas Vermaelen (formerly Arsenal) and Divock Origi (Liverpool).

Of course, such revolution requires investment. But if countries like Belgium and Iceland can do it, then why should Ireland settle for second best? And why should we not dream of better times when foreign observers might talk about the technical ability of Irish players and not just the undying spirit and togetherness of the national side?

Positively, Dokter seems open to developing Irish football along a similar model, if not an exact replica, of the Belgian way.

And his passion for the development of skill from a young age, against the importance of winning matches, will be a key issue in the plan, as Dokter envisages that 11-a-side matches on full-sized pitches should not be introduced until U13 level.

There are also plans to establish FAI-approved underage football academies in local clubs and to create continuity of football by shifting to a one-season calendar from March to November.

Since the plan was announced, the critics – never far away in Irish football – have had their say. And the proposed switch to a more summer-based playing calendar has been high on the list of concerns.

Critics of the plan fear that going head-to-head with other sporting codes, namely the traditional national game Gaelic football, could be detrimental to the future of many schoolboy clubs, particularly those in rural communities where Gaelic football and hurling are more popular sporting pursuits.

The FAI cannot turn a blind eye to these concerns and they should take all opinions on board. And they should speak to concerned parties about their worries. But that, as far as I would be concerned, is as far as the FAI should go.

For in my opinion, the FAI cannot afford to show weakness in pushing through controversial parts of the plan. They must be relentless in the pursuit of long-term goals and cannot bow to outside pressure. The notion that you can 'keep everybody happy' is useless in football. And has anybody ever heard of a quiet and bloodless revolution, where everyone remains friends? It doesn't happen.

Summer soccer, for example, is an absolute must if Ireland is to produce better technical players. And why put obstacles in the way, like worrying whether players will choose Gaelic football over football? Why not embrace the proposal and approach it with a fresh and open mind? In my view, it should be utterly irrelevant, anyway, what happens in other codes. You just wish them (those involved in other codes) the very best and carry on with your own lot.

For example, in recent years summer football has blossomed in Mayo, a Gaelic football hotbed in the west of Ireland. And despite summer football going well, it hasn't impacted on the success of Mayo's Gaelic football sides. I don't understand why both codes cannot run smoothly.

I just don't buy the assumption that summer football provides a messy culture clash between codes. Is it not possible for both sides to be content?

In any case, if the plan is carried out then underage games will be more about player development than winning matches. Therefore, I ask if it's really detrimental when a promising young player opts for a different code, be it Gaelic football, rugby or chess?

Does their decision to focus on another sport not confirm that they never had the desire anyway to become a top footballer? Are youth coaches not better knowing that from an early stage? Or is it better to invest enormous amounts of time and energy developing a young player, for six or seven years, only to see the player disregard football in his teens?

For if a mentality can be fostered where coaches are no longer infatuated with winning – an infatuation even prevalent in U6 and U7 football – should it really matter, in the long term, if one of their strongest boys chooses to play Gaelic football?

If the child never had the desire to be a footballer, despite possessing some of the strengths to do so, then coaches have to move on and work on transforming 'good' young players into 'great' young players. That is where the best youth coaches earn their reputations, by taking flimsy, flawed materials and eventually turning them to pure silk.

Crucially, the introduction of summer-based seasons would lead to better playing and training surfaces and provide more regular training and playing time for Ireland's young generations of footballers. There would be less of those frustrating winter morning cancellations due to frost, wind and rain. And the children would get far more regular football. And that's surely what we need. For it stands to reason that players will try constructing better passing moves in better conditions, thus giving them more touches of the ball per match and, as a result, they hopefully foster better technique and game understanding.

Personally, I have reported on many schoolboy matches in the last 20 years and sometimes, to be frank, it has been downright cruel asking young players, sometimes below ten years old, to impress in horrible wintry conditions.

Farcically, the strength of the wind, in one half of the game, can often decide the final outcome, as one team valiantly battle through the first half with the wind in their face to painfully find that the direction of the gale has altered in the second half.

These utterly barmy occurrences need banishing from Irish schoolboy football. Furthermore, wouldn't it be wonderful to see indoor futsal leagues run all over the country every week or two in the winter months, to keep children bright and focused on the game and their ongoing development?

So, while that is the ultimate dream for some, it is also a long way down the road, according to former Arsenal and Ireland striker Graham Barrett.

'I think the senior team are doing unbelievably well. Our management team [Martin O'Neill and Roy Keane] are exceptional. We have some fantastic players in terms of their heart, their character, their desire, their commitment to doing well for Ireland – and obviously their talent, as well. What they're doing is inspiring, but it's also buying us time because there is a lot to be done at youth level. People shouldn't think, all of a sudden, "we're okay". There's an awful lot of work to be done. It would be incredibly naive to think the opposite,' Barrett told an Irish website in 2016.

'When I was away in the summer [2016], watching the games in France in the European Championships, what hit you is how incredibly together the Irish fans were. We get called the best fans in the world, and they are. They're so far ahead of every other country in terms of sticking together, sticking by the team. But when you come home, domestically, grass roots and the organisations around the country that facilitate the game, nothing could be further from the truth. We're not together. It's incredibly divisive. That's what we need to produce – a conveyor belt [of talent]. And that can only start if every organisation in the country starts working together. You've got to strike a balance and you won't unless everyone works together. That still hasn't happened.

'I met Ruud Dokter. We sat down for two hours and had a chat. I found him very sincere and he's trying his best. But the people behind him need to give him the power and support to implement what he wants to implement. But not all of the associations that govern football in Ireland play nice together. That's a real problem.

'There are things that I didn't agree with Ruud on, and I voiced that, and he voiced his opinion. We had a very honest conversation. I felt within that two hours that he had the best interests of Irish football [at heart], but if he's to implement his ideas – if we're to build on the brilliant work that Martin O'Neill and Roy Keane and the team have done in the last year – everyone is going to have to start working together. And unless that happens, we'll find ourselves in real trouble again, in a year, or two years, or three or four years… whenever it may be, but it will happen,' adds Barrett.

So, while it is intriguing to consider Irish youth football and its structures in a different light, where harmony and co-operation run through its core, it remains painfully evident, from listening to Barrett and others who have voiced concerns about the state of the game, that radical change is not going to happen today or tomorrow. In fact, it could be several decades before an Irish senior manager can properly reap the reward of Dokter's labour.

And while I have been reliably informed that Dokter is a fine man to drive the youth ship, I, for one, would feel a lot more optimistic had Brian Kerr, as outlined at the beginning of this chapter, been chosen to take Irish football forward as the high performance director; a view shared by one of the country's most dynamic ever wingers, Damien Duff, who played a starring role for Kerr's successful Ireland youth sides.

'The passion he brought [to the Ireland set-up] could always get an extra ten per cent or 20 per cent out of us,' Duff says.

'He talked about being a proud Irishman and how your family and friends are back home thinking about you. We used to be in tears, literally, going out on the pitch. He got us to 12th or something in the world. If it wasn't for two goals against Israel, home and away, which was nothing to do with him, we would have won the group to qualify for the 2006 World Cup. I just can't fathom how he is not involved in Irish football. He is on TV and he does a bit of radio. You name any footballer in the world, and he'll tell you about them now.

'His knowledge of the game is second to none,' adds the former Chelsea star.

Thereby, what you have is a former Premier League title winner with huge international experience and a deep understanding of the game championing Brian Kerr's cause. Do the powers-that-be in Abbotstown possess greater football acumen than the likes of Duff, or many others who acknowledge that Kerr's loss to Irish football is something approaching a national disaster?

For me, Kerr has the exact tools to ensure the overall focus in youth coaching switches from the win-at-all-costs mentality to developing more technically adept and skilful players.

Ireland has always been okay at producing physical players full of endeavour and heart and while there have been exceptions to the trend, like the magnificent Liam Brady and Paul McGrath, Ireland has traditionally toiled in developing absolutely outstanding technical players.

For this to occur more often, change will have to come. And wouldn't it be most wonderful if Brian Kerr, a man who has already dedicated an entire life to guiding young Irish footballers, could be involved in the revolution, in some capacity?

Chapter 7

The Kids Are Not Alright

I N many ways these are different times we are living in. Society has changed; not just in Ireland but pretty much everywhere around Europe. Our ways have changed. The way we communicate with each other is different. And the way young people behave and interact has been altered, dramatically.

And despite claims that there have never been more young people playing football, you sometimes wonder where these youngsters actually are!

In Ireland currently, there are empty fields and patches of grass where once young people played with abandon and goodwill.

Yet, on the other side of the world, if you trawl the backstreets and sand pitches of South America, football-hungry youngsters are playing football, everywhere. There, they hone their first touch, close ball control and clever movement and their insatiable appetite for the game. They play day in and day out. They cannot get enough of it. They love their football and see it, crucially, as a way to a better life. They crave the game and also its potential personal rewards.

If you look around some of Europe's top leagues, you will see South Americans at the heart of the continent's leading club competitions. The South American children have heroes aplenty and they are playing in every leading European league. And South American children, often from poor backgrounds, do everything possible to emulate those idols.

But do Irish children, or even British children, have the same desire to be the best? Do they have the will or heart to practise and practise and then practise again? Are they prepared to give blood, sweat and tears to triumph? And are they willing to get in the local park for a kick-about with friends; the kind that for years was the cornerstone on which great players built their technical and physical skills?

The brilliant former England winger Chris Waddle, who enjoyed a wonderful spell in French football for Marseille, which really proved what a technical talent he was, has spoken in the past about the need for English football to return to basics, and enable children to start enjoying the game again. Waddle, who won 62 England caps, was a terrific winger, who became known for dropping his shoulder before skinning his marker with consummate ease. And when he looks at the modern game, he told the exceptional journalist Graham Hunter, he sees regimented players incapable of producing the kind of magical moments that made him famous.

Waddle believes that British players have lost the ability to think for themselves on the pitch and that the current academy system, in England, does no favours for encouraging creativity and on-field dynamism. Waddle also tells the story (in Hunter's enthralling podcast series, 'The Big Interview') of learning the game, as a young teenager, against grown men. He said the experience of playing against older and sometimes more crude opponents taught him quickly the skills and movement that would serve him brilliantly in his elite career. Can you imagine, these days, if a young teenager was fielded against players ten or 15 years his senior? There would be an outcry.

We have to ask if Irish and European society, as a whole, has become too wishy-washy for its own good. The Arsenal manager Arsène Wenger believes so and says that the culture makes British football unable to nurture 'fighters' like in South America. Indeed, when the England national team crashed out of the 2016 European Championships with a whimper, the former Liverpool stalwart Jamie Carragher described the players as too soft and pampered. In most cases they just don't have the balls for the battle, unlike the South Americans, who can outplay opponents with cunning and guile, but also fight them like dogs when needs must.

For evidence of what South America continues to produce, compared to Ireland and Great Britain, one only has to look at the top clubs in Europe. In Spain, for example, the South Americans always had huge influence, going back to the glory days of Hector Rial, Jose Santamaria and Alfredo di Stefano, as Real Madrid won five straight European Cups in the 1950s.

These days, Real Madrid's main influences come from Europe. Yet their fiercest rivals, FC Barcelona, have a strong core of South Americans in their fantastic side.

Having once been the playing field of the great Diego Maradona before he departed for a wonderful spell with Napoli, the Camp Nou is now enthralled, week after week, by the fascinating artistry and industry of attacking duo Lionel Messi and Luis Suárez, who were ably assisted in the Blaugrana attrack by Brazilian Neymar before his mega-money transfer to Paris Saint-Germain in the summer of 2017.

They are blessed with the most sublime technique and Messi, the little Argentinian wizard, is regarded, by many, as the greatest footballer in the history of the game. But what do Messi, Neymar and Suárez have in common? Their South American backgrounds, of course. They all hailed from humble beginnings but had the passion, skill and desire to make it to the top. While the mesmeric Messi, these days, has some pedestrian moments (while always staying alert to space around him), Neymar and Suárez, from Brazil and Uruguay respectively, have hugely admirable work ethics, particularly in the case of the latter, who is well known for his immense contributions for Liverpool.

Okay, Suárez often allows his temper to get the better of his judgement. He has a questionable disciplinary record and was involved in one too many regrettable on-field incidents. But Suárez is also an inspiration; full of running, determination and a steely desire to win. But most importantly, he is a team player in every sense of the expression. He works enormously hard for the team and yet always has the composure and physical strength to punish opponents by sticking the ball in the net.

For any young striker looking to play as a centre-forward, there are many fine examples in the modern game. But are any of them as heroic as Suárez; a real fighter on the pitch and a player of clever, incisive movement and wonderful ability? They are joined in the Barcelona ranks by the Argentine Javier Mascherano, who again displays many of the characteristics missing in some current European players: an unbelievable toughness, sheer grit and will to win, and a superb understanding of where he ought to be on the pitch.

Indeed, they are far from the first South Americans to light up the famous Camp Nou, where Brazilians Rivaldo, Romario and Ronaldinho often carried the team, like compatriot Ronaldo (Brazil) did before. Ronaldo, of course, also performed magically in a five-year spell at Real Madrid.

But the aforementioned South American trio are not alone in flying the South American flag in Europe. The South Americans are everywhere where beautiful football, and winning football, is played.

In Italy, Juventus have won the last six Serie A championships with Argentine Paulo Dybala and Chilean Arturo Vidal (who has since helped Bayern Munich continue their domination in Germany) in the side. Others to help The Old Lady's cause in recent seasons included Dani Alves (a former Barcelona hero), Juan Cuadrado, Gonzalo Higuaín and Alex Sandro. The Uruguayan Edinson Cavani and Brazilian team-mate Thiago Silva, formerly of AC Milan in Italy, are leading the revolution at Paris Saint-Germain, in France, while English football has seen its fair share of South American class in the guise of Alexis Sanchez (formerly of Barcelona) and Willian.

Sanchez, like Luis Suárez and Edinson Cavani, consistently displays the hard-working, street-fighting South American values that often make their continent's players stand out. But where are these same values and strengths in our own modern players?

For example, when I was growing up on an Irish housing estate in the 1980s, playing football was all that mattered. But could you honestly say the same about today's kids?

Back then it was jumpers for goalposts and we would play, hyper-enthusiastic, for hours on end. You literally couldn't wait to get started. And you never wanted to end. After school we would dash home as quickly as possible, throw our uniforms on the floor (much to mother's chagrin) and get our tracksuits on.

Of course, we were entering a time, in the late 1980s, when supporting and playing football was more popular than ever before in Ireland. Boosted by the international team qualifying for its first ever major tournaments in 1988 and 1990, football had finally emerged from the background and its second fiddle status to Gaelic football and hurling, to suddenly become a sport that brought an entire nation together. The Irish players and manager Jack Charlton became gods to the Irish people. And everyone seemed to want a piece of the action.

For me, playing and watching the game was everything. Yet it took the incredible success of Jack Charlton's Boys in Green to provide the platform for Irish football to grow, especially in terms of increasing the number of children participating.

Thankfully, there was always ample green space in our park – and one about 20 yards from my front door bang in the middle of a football-obsessed estate. And so, it was a very short walk across the road, from house to green, where my friends assembled ready for battle in our very own Wembley Stadium. That is how it felt, for me. Every little match or every game of heads and volleys was like the World Cup Final. You enjoyed it. But you were also, unknowingly, developing your skill and the will to win.

Gleefully, we would spend a couple of hours playing, imagining ourselves to be the stars of the English First Division (before the advent of the Premier League in the early 1990s). And when called ashore by mother, for homework or dinner, such laborious distractions were consumed and completed at the speed of light. To us, getting back on the park was all that mattered. Algebra and Pythagoras could wait another day. But running, tackling, sweating, passing, scoring and savouring every kick-about could not.

As quickly as possible, it was back outside; getting plenty of touches of the ball, trying new skills and learning all the time. We were developing, almost unknown to ourselves. We just lived for it.

Indeed, football made my week, as a child. It still does (perhaps somewhat sadly). But the game, for me, is magical. There's always the next game to look forward to. The analysis of what transpired in the week before. And there is always a next hurdle for your team to climb.

In school, I constantly daydreamed about the spectacular performance I hoped my favourite team might produce in their next game. And I would recap, over and over in my head, how they managed to win, lose or draw the previous match. All the while, I couldn't wait to get home to play. It just meant everything and more, but sadly I don't see that innocent passion in most modern children.

And when we (my friends and I) were not playing, which was rare indeed, we talked about the game or collected and swapped the old Panini football stickers. They were rare times and the best of times.

The players we saw on television – only once a week, if you were lucky – were heroes and inspirations. But it was different then. We just idolised footballers for what they were – footballers. Unlike today's children who seem more interested in copying hairstyles of football's star players.

The kids seem to know the boot sponsors of the top players. But do they scrutinise what the players actually do with the boots? Do they look closely at movement and technique? Do they assess what to do out of possession, or do they notice the tactics deployed by each team?

In the 1980s, we certainly didn't know or care about players' big fancy cars and houses, and we most definitely didn't give a fiddler's about wives and girlfriends. Instead, we just copied their skill on the pitch.

Football, indeed, had dominated my thoughts back then – and some might say that not much has changed.

Such was the level of my childhood obsession that I vividly remember one of my schoolteachers scornfully remarking that 'O'Neill can't tell us the bloody answer [to a mathematics question] but can tell us who is bottom of the Fourth Division!'

He wasn't wrong either. And I swiftly informed him that Aldershot were rock bottom of the English Football League. Sure, who needs maths when that type of utter jargon runs through the brain?

In a way, my friends and I were lucky to be raised on a genuine football estate, where a number of enthusiastic and well qualified coaches lived. Thankfully, our coaches – including Pauric Nicholson, who progressed to be one of the country's finest coaches and coach tutors – happened to love the game as much as we did (and possibly even more), so playing in our area was never a problem (even if the house window suffered along the way).

Pauric, at the time, was an avid promoter of the Coerver Coaching method. And only lately, I listened to an interview with the former England striker Peter Crouch, in which he recalls attending special Coerver training camps in England. Crouch told of how the Coerver method gave him many of the tools that took him to the top of his profession. As kids, Pauric would have us clued in to certain aspects of Coerver.

And as a goalkeeper, I remember Pauric always telling me to go home after training to watch the former Ajax, Juventus and Manchester United net minder Edwin van der Sar. He didn't want me watching van der Sar's handling techniques. Or the Dutchman's shot-stopping. No, he wanted me to learn how to be comfortable with the ball at my feet.

It wasn't long after the introduction of the back-pass rule and Pauric believed that van der Sar was the best around at playing out from the back. I listened to him and subsequently learned. Kids these days though, do they listen to that sort of vital direction?

Crucially, our desire to play never waned. It was bred in our way of thinking and indeed, I remember training in some awful conditions, including the snow after only six players showed up (probably certain that Pauric would cancel the session). There was no chance. And it turned out to be a most enjoyable session.

But would that sort of thing happen today? Because if you look in the parks and green areas in Ireland's villages, towns and cities, one cannot fail to wonder where all the young footballers have gone?

There seems, to me, to be very few children, if any at all, playing the game in the street or the local parks. It is a major and concerning problem. For example, where I have lived for ten years, a housing estate in central Ireland, there is one major green area. It surrounds a pond that was once home to a number of fish and frogs, which always provided much entertainment for the neighbourhood's young children. But the fish and beady-eyed comrades are long gone, as their residence became neglected. As for the green area enveloping it, well it sits largely unused.

And it's not like there's a shortage of young people in the area to utilise it. No, the number of youths in the area is not in question. They are plentiful. But they don't play football there. In fact, they don't seem to play football anywhere – apart from with local schoolboy clubs.

It seems most children are playing the game only in organised settings, whether once a week, in training for their clubs (for an hour or so), or when representing clubs in weekend matches. Aside from that, they are glued to phones and other modern devices.

So, the kids might be playing, occasionally. But it is nowhere near enough; a fact pointed out by former Millwall and Ireland player Eamon Dunphy, who has long lamented the state of the modern game.

'Soccer, as we've known it, is dead,' Dunphy proclaimed in a radio interview in early 2016.

'The game is dying everywhere because it's not being played on the streets. It's an old refrain, but true. It's an international problem but for us [in Ireland] it's nearly terminal,' he adds.

Whether or not Ireland's current predicament is that bad is open to debate. And it would be wildly inaccurate to suggest that the country doesn't have some outstanding young coaches. But what is not open to disagreement, at all, is the glaring number of side-attractions tempting kids away from once busy green fields.

Computers, social media, iPhones, television and a host of other non-sporting pastimes have become a strain on the youth's physical and mental well-being and development.

In 2014, for example, pre-orders for the new Sony PlayStation 4 console were higher in Ireland compared to any other country in the world, according to a comparison of GameStop global pre-order sales. At roughly the same time, Ireland led the way on a worldwide scale for pre-orders of the Microsoft Xbox One – only behind Australia. These figures alone tell a story about the priorities of many of the country's children.

Ironically though, some of the most played computer games relate to football with EA Sports' 'FIFA 17' and 'Pro Evolution Soccer' (Konami) proving insanely popular with people around the world. Some have suggested that taking part in these games, where the graphics and latest developments take you to a realm of fantasy that seems so real, is the closest that some aspiring footballers will ever get to competing against and 'playing alongside' real-life superstars like Lionel Messi and Cristiano Ronaldo. And fair enough, that might be true in some respect.

But surely, if taking part in surreal activities becomes more important than actually training and playing with mates, then something is wrong?

Of course, we all dabbled in some form of computer game escapism – some more than others. For me, there was a lengthy period when the popular 'Football Manager' game (Sega) took over a large chunk of my life. Indeed, its popularity has even spawned a book in its honour, *Football Manager Stole My Life* by Iain Macintosh, Kenny Millar and Neil White.

'Football Manager' does what it says on the tin; allowing you (the player) to take charge of practically any football club in the world, from Real Madrid to Cabinteely. It gives the player control of almost every facet of the club from balancing transfer budgets to signing and selling players to choosing team formations and tactics. It can, no doubt, be a fascinating and empowering virtual experience.

For example, I remember building a smashing Dundee United side in one version of the game, maybe 15 years ago; helping the Tangerines to topple the all-powerful Old Firm and enjoy European success. For a time I really enjoyed it. And these games are quite consuming. Easily, you find yourself going over formations and potential new signings in your head, as you become immersed in your 'managerial' role.

All of a sudden, you are searching Google for 'Football Manager's Most Exciting Young Players' or 'Football Manager's Best Bargains', as you try to sneak ahead of the game. But it rarely worked for me, and to the best of my memory, frustration was usually the name of the game in 'Football Manager'. But it was somewhat addictive.

Look, games like this can be enjoyable. They pass the time. And its players could certainly be dabbling in worse pastimes. Yet ultimately, they are merely spin-offs of the real thing. And for children, these games contribute to a widespread reluctance to get on the local park and play football, the real way. It means that many children are missing the fresh air pelting against their skin and muck gradually etching its way on their hands and legs. They don't experience the innocent and wonderful joy of doing something extraordinary on the pitch; of having fun with friends and pursuing a healthy activity along the way. Instead, they are cocooned in heated bedrooms, engaging in pastimes that keep them occupied but at what long-term cost?

Indeed, when speaking to schoolchildren at an event organised by former Manchester United team-mate Pat McGibbon in 2016, Irish football legend Roy Keane, now the national team assistant manager, told young footballers to get rid of the various electronic devices and concentrate on enjoying the game.

'Throw them [mobile phones] in the bin, throw them in the bin,' Keane says. 'Play football, practice. Kick the ball against the wall, play with your mates. Kids don't climb trees any more. So that's my advice, enjoy football and climb trees,' Keane adds.

Maybe some people could interpret Keane's comments as over the top. Yet, it is clear that he has strong views on the matter and is, in this writer's opinion, pretty close to the mark, as children undoubtedly spend considerably more time in front of computer consoles than pursuing physical fulfilment – whether through football or a plethora of other sports on offer.

As a result, Irish children appear to be suffering the consequences of leading inactive childhoods and indeed, at a presentation on the subject of childhood obesity in 2014, Dr Sinead Murphy, a paediatrician in Temple Street Children's Hospital, said that 40 per cent of children seen at the hospital's specialist obesity clinic display withdrawn behaviour and psychological difficulties. The same number of children treated at the clinic had high cholesterol, Dr Murphy reported. Furthermore, Dr Murphy highlighted how an overweight or obese ten-year-old has a more than 80 per cent chance of becoming an overweight or obese adult.

'In young clients it would be almost the norm that they would be in tears when asked if people tease them about their weight,' she says.

And today, in Ireland, it's estimated that about one in four children are either overweight or obese with fewer than 50 per cent getting the required amount of exercise (60 minutes per day).

Not competing in sport, of course, is not the only reason for young people becoming overweight, obese or psychologically troubled. But it can certainly be a contributing factor.

Yet the mantra from the Football Association of Ireland (FAI) remains that more children are playing football than any other sport, despite most experts in youth coaching admitting that young Irish players don't get enough coaching from a young age and training facilities have lagged behind other nations for some time.

Speaking in early 2016, former Arsenal player Graham Barrett said there are huge issues in Irish football's grassroots/underage levels and that Ireland will never again produce the likes of Liam Brady, John Giles, Roy Keane and Paul McGrath unless drastic and urgent action is taken.

'As things stand,' he says, 'the simple truth is that the technical and physical standard of the majority of young players in Ireland will continue to steadily decrease unless we act and tackle the issues dramatically. It's imperative we open our eyes and recognise that we have drastically fallen behind our rivals.'

But what is so wrong with the structures? And if the system was so bad for so long, how come Brady, Giles, Keane and McGrath made it to the top? Social changes, Barrett says, are largely to blame.

'Players of generations past were out kicking a ball on the street as soon as they got home from school until well after dark,' says Barrett. 'There is absolutely still a love for football in society and many children still dream of becoming footballers. But there are so many more distractions that kids just are not playing enough street football any more. They have become more reliant on their limited practice time at clubs to allow them to improve, rather than the self-educated street football greats of our past,' adds Barrett, who played six times for Ireland until persistent injury problems led to his retirement.

'Our structures are outdated and have been failing us for a long time,' he continues. 'Put simply, we have stagnated while the football world has moved on. We stood back and watched as other countries professionalised themselves in how they developed players from an earlier age and invested in new facilities. As measures were implemented elsewhere to increase the numbers of properly qualified coaches, we did next to nothing.'

All over Europe, Barrett explains, aspiring young footballers aged between eight and 12 train between eight and 12 hours a week, while players aged 12 to 16 can practise as much as 12 to 15 hours a week at 'fantastic training facilities' before entering full-time environments at professional clubs, if deemed good enough.

'Here,' he says, 'our kids get an hour on a Tuesday and Thursday, on very poor surfaces more fit for a local gang piss-up than a technical football session. With just that in mind, how in God's name do we expect to continue to keep pace with other countries unless we radically change our approach?' he adds.

Just like in Iceland, you could say, where the Football Association has completely reshaped football in the last 15 years through widespread investment in indoor and all-weather pitches.

But as importantly, they also pumped resources into producing vast quantities of qualified coaches. And now, in a country with fewer than 330,000 inhabitants, Iceland has almost 650 qualified coaches (almost one for every 500 people).

And while the FAI emerging talent programme that brings together the cream of schoolboy talent at various training centres across the country has its supporters, there are those who feel that it only scratches the surface in the bid to mould potential Premier League stars.

'It requires time to install measures to improve the volume and standard of our coaching,' says Barrett.

'But the plans put in place so far are just not good enough. For example, the emerging talent programmes do not provide enough training time. Indeed, the drawn-out development plan to improve grass-roots football in

Ireland is only so-so and although some parts are good, overall it fails to scratch the surface in terms of establishing the foundation we need to put in place before we can kick on,' he claims.

Furthermore, I argue, where has the fun gone in youth football?

Are we seeing enough children given an allowance, in training and matches, to freely express their skill?

What I usually see, in underage football, is teams and players put in a certain system of play, usually 4-3-3, with a total lack of flexibility to create something magical, something a bit different that breaks the system. It is actually quite sad seeing a young player releasing the ball, pass backwards or to the nearest team-mate, when they evidently have the capacity to do something more creative; to maybe take an opponent on with trickery and close ball control. For it's a beautiful thing seeing young players drop their shoulder to go past an opponent or try an audacious flick or back-heel in the hope of manufacturing a rare eye-opening incident in otherwise dour and rigid contests. There is no spontaneity in the play; nothing different.

Occasionally, you come across coaches who encourage more freedom and expression. But in Ireland, I don't think it's happening anywhere near enough. What this means, ultimately, is that we produce the same kind of player over and over again. And it means our players usually lack creativity and the ability to stand out in a crowd. The young players cannot be blamed. If they are not encouraged to express themselves from an early age and are constantly told to not be selfish or extravagant with the ball, then where has the fun gone? Why can we not let them loose; let them enjoy themselves and smooth out the deficiencies later on?

Young players, it seems, are rarely encouraged to showcase individual skill and are told to 'clear the ball' or 'get rid of it' at the soonest possible moment; increasing the risk of losing possession and increasing the likelihood of conceding a goal. And this can happen from U7 level up! So, is it any wonder that so many children turn their back on the game in their teens, almost too afraid of coaches to continue on?

Indeed, John Devine, the former Arsenal defender who works valiantly in schoolboy football, told the *Irish Examiner* newspaper that Irish football has to act quickly to solve its various problems.

'There are great volunteers putting time into the game all around the country,' he reflects, 'but we need leadership to say "this is the way we're going to play from this age". And that has to come from the FAI. It wouldn't cost a fortune. The FAI need to make the decision and take it by the scruff of the neck. We don't have time to waste and need to get into this now. When you look at other countries' underage teams that we play against – technically they're miles ahead; the Spanish, the Germans, all way, way ahead. The Belgians now are going to reap the rewards of a ten-year plan going back to the drawing board. And unless we do something we're going to get left behind. Kids are naturally competitive but they can't win with the wrong fundamentals. The Irish mentality is to win, win, win at all costs from the youngest age upwards on pitches and with goals that, as we know, are too big.

'I want to win in everything I do too, but the children first need to learn how to win. Instead, we have someone who thinks he's a manager or a coach trying to play systems and shapes and then he's screaming his head off at the weekend because the kids can't control the ball. So, we really have the cart before the horse. We need to get back to the fundamentals, work on the kids' touch, control and passing and then when they do go into games they're prepared to play the game the right way.'

But until the Irish coaching system, and training facilities across the country, are improved significantly (which could still be a long way down the road) the Ireland senior team will continue its reliance on the English academy system to put the finishing touches to its most decent young players. And to an extent, the national side will continue relying on recruiting players who qualify for the team but who were born in England – 50 years on from the first non-Irish-born player (Shay Brennan) pulling on the green shirt.

Ten years later (1975), Ireland (under player-manager John Giles) fielded a side comprised solely of Irish-born players in a qualifying match for the 1976 European Championships. On that occasion, Limerick's Don Givens – the only player from outside Dublin – scored a hat-trick as Ireland brushed Turkey aside, 4-0.

But with the troubles that seem to exist in the Irish underage system, it's unlikely that Ireland will ever be able to field another all-Irish-born side.

'I don't think it's feasible, at least not soon,' says Irish football writer Trevor Murray.

'Of course, anything is possible given time, but with a country like the Republic of Ireland, it is hard to see the national side ever fielding a team made up entirely of Republic-born players,' he adds.

However, instead of seeing this as some form of negative for the country, Murray sees things very differently.

'Aside from the obvious issues of population size, competing against other sports like Gaelic games and rugby means that soccer always has a more intense fight on its hands to attract players than similarly sized countries. There is also the fact that it makes sense for the senior team and the subsequent age brackets for underage set-ups to search far and wide for talent.

The international scene, no more than the club stage, has become incredibly competitive over the years and whether it's Martin O'Neill or the next Irish boss in the senior hot-seat, they are always going to scour the globe for exciting talent – firstly because they are well within their rights to do so and secondly, because if it means finding the next Damien Duff or Robbie Keane then they will pursue it as actively as they can, even if the player wasn't born in Ireland.

Players eligible to play for Ireland can be found all over the world, if you do your research and look hard enough, so it makes sense that those avenues are explored. For example, there's a teenager playing for Bayern Munich in Germany who was born to a Swedish father and Irish mother in Luxembourg. Ryan Johansson is his name. He's a highly rated kid with bags of ability – that's how multicultural the game has become. There are surely many others out there just like him, good players learning their trade at big European clubs and getting a world-class football education along the way. Why shouldn't these guys be looked at?

'For me, it shouldn't be a case of harking back to the so-called glory days when the national team could field a side wholly comprised of Irish-born players; it should be about constructing and coaching a team so that they can compete with the best – no matter where they were born. As far as I'm concerned, if they're eligible to play and they're happy to pull on the green jersey, then that's who the scouts and coaches should be looking to bring in,' he says.

But at the very least, insists fellow writer Miguel Delaney, young players in Ireland simply must be given better opportunities to improve. He also suggests that people involved in Irish football must begin to set higher standards.

'In theory, there should be no reason why Irish football cannot do what Spain, Germany and so many other countries have done on our own scale. The question is whether that is actually possible in reality. If Germany have put in place the perfect football structure, Spain the finest coaching, and Belgium and Holland have found a way to apply both for smaller countries, Ireland still remain some way off such ideals.

'The framework ensures we still produce a competitive international team by accident rather than design, despite some admirable changes to coaching across the spectrum. Quite simply, the current structure is not making efficient use of the talent that is there. Irish football remains hugely dependent on English clubs to finish the coaching of players older than 16,' says the author of *Stuttgart to Saipan: the Players' Stories*.

His namesake (and no relation) John Delaney, the FAI chief executive officer, continues to push the notion that Ireland has a bright future, both in underage and senior international football.

'We are at a crucial time for the development of our sport, particularly in the area of elite player development,' he said in a briefing report on the FAI Player Development Plan.

'But I know that if everybody in the football family pulls together as one team we can deliver good results. By working together with an open mind and putting the players first, we can all play our part in raising the standards of our game across Ireland. It is now very apparent that standards are rising across the world and we want to ensure that we are not left behind. We want to see Ireland teams for long into the future playing in World Cups and UEFA European Championships, and we want to see our underage international sides regularly qualifying for the major tournaments,' he added.

Sadly, Mr Delaney, your association hasn't ensured that Ireland is not left behind. That ship has sailed, I'm afraid, and Ireland is already playing an almighty game of catch-up on its European rivals.

And although young Irish players like Conor Masterson (Liverpool), Ismael Diallo (Nottingham Forest), Zachary Elbouzedi (West Bromwich Albion), Avis Ganiyu (Sunderland), Daniel Mandroiu (Brighton & Hove Albion) and Jean Yves Poame (Sunderland) seem to have a chance to forge good careers in England, there can be no arguing that the disjointed Irish way of schooling young players is grotesquely outdated and needs revamping, if we are to reap the rewards at senior international level.

The country's future success can only be dictated by, and built on, a rock solid, imaginative and creative formula for producing high quality. The FAI might argue that a creative formula was introduced with the Player Development Plan. But just like Mr Delaney's words about 'football families' and 'elite player development', formulating a plan is very different to putting it in proper motion. Talk is very cheap in life, and even cheaper in football. It's only actions that will grab the attention of football people. And Irish football has been sadly lacking in that regard in the last number of decades.

And until the talking stops and actions take over, Irish people will simply continue to kid themselves that the occasional positive international result suggests that there's no huge problems in the overall structure when, clearly, the complete opposite rings true.

Conclusion

The Road to Fame
Or Failure?

WILL we ever find the Irish of old – those great star players that return to Ireland, on retiring, not with stories of regret and disappointment but bagfuls of medals and golden memories? Or has the cause of Irish players in England reached a point of no return? Are they now a spent force in English football and can they ever again reach the top?

These are questions that ran through my mind having concluded my research and interviews for this book. And although it is impossible to be definitive on the future, I feel that people involved in Irish football really need to start finding workable and realistic solutions to the many difficulties facing our game. But what can be done, you ask?

For is it not just part of our football culture for our best young players to always go to England – and to be largely disappointed? Is it not virtually impossible to alter this trend? Indeed, the challenge of changing the mentality of Irish people in relation to sending our young players to England, in search of fame and fortune, would be absolutely massive. But surely, there have to be positive steps we can take to stem the tide of battered and bruised youngsters returning to Ireland, having not made the grade, who then struggle to integrate back into the game on home soil?

Firstly, it would be helpful if Irish people could rearrange their collective thoughts on the relationship between our young players and English football. Doing so would be a mightily difficult task, especially now that the monetary rewards in England have become so vast. In that sense, Irish football will never be able to compete.

But what we can do is to gradually convince young players and their parents/guardians that there can be a more trusted pathway to long-term success by staying in Ireland, rather than jumping across the pond to join the first big English club to come calling.

In that regard, the introduction of National Leagues at U15, U17 and U19 levels is a step in the right direction. There are also plans to have a National League at U13s. Immediately, these steps have provided organised, gradual steps for progression in League of Ireland clubs; steps that previously had not been there.

As always, there is opposition to those moves. And some schoolboy league clubs and coaches probably feel aggrieved, in some ways, at allowing their best young players to join League of Ireland clubs before they hit their teens. Their concerns, however, are based on the track record of League of Ireland clubs not looking after young players. And that, it must be said, is a fair concern to have.

But I feel the outlook of League of Ireland clubs, and the environment in which they now operate, is not as disorganised and chaotic as before. Okay, certain clubs are still struggling to survive on a week to week basis. But most league clubs have adopted a more prudent approach to finances in recent years, and become more than aware that their future existence lies in the hands of youth development, as opposed to signing a raft of journeymen on an annual basis only to find yourself repeating the vicious cycle at the start of every season when they get a better financial offer elsewhere. The league has certainly become a young man's game. There were times in the past when physicality and brute strength were the main requirements for playing in the league. In the 1990s, for example, when I started really getting interested in the league and learning what type of players were required to build a solid outfit, it seemed that the meaner and more grotesque you were, the better player you were, too.

But that way of building teams has gone. And in more recent years the league has become more about sprightly, hungry, fit and technically assured players. Now, there is still room for the tough, unruly type. It is not La Liga after all.

However, if you compare today's league with the 1980s or 1990s, the dissimilarity between them is enormous. Indeed, a few years ago I was speaking with a former league midfielder, who was in the course of watching a league match, and he claimed the league was unrecognisable from the one he played in in the 1980s and 1990s. For him, it seemed like a different game altogether. No longer were midfielders and defenders crunching into tackles and blatantly using elbows to smash opponents.

And playing the 'percentages', where teams under pressure just launch the ball into empty spaces to allow them to move up the field, was a thing of the past. He was taken aback to see so much passing football. Now again, we need to put this into context. We are not talking about the free-flowing passing of Europe's top teams. And don't get me wrong, the League of Ireland in the 1980s and 1990s had some wonderful silky players; like Liam Coyle, Paul Doolin, Pat Fenlon, Patsy Freyne, Paul Osam and Tony Sheridan. These were diamonds in the rough, masters of the ball and creators-in-chief.

But what we see now, most definitely, is the emergence of slighter players who might have been lost in times gone by. They are energetic and, in some cases, more savvy about their bodies and how to reach optimum fitness levels. Many club facilities are slowly improving, strength and conditioning is getting there, and the actual quality of the players in the league is fairly strong. The recent European success of Dundalk has also given the league a massive boost, and given their players huge exposure outside the island. And their success, along with many other improvements in the domestic league, is gradually convincing many young players that staying at home, until their early 20s could be the way forward in the future.

These players have huge examples to follow, starting with the current Republic of Ireland captain Seamus Coleman. The Donegal right-back was playing for his local club St Catherine's, aged 17, when he impressed Sligo Rovers in a friendly match. From there, he signed a contract worth €130 a week and started training full time, five days a week.

In an interview for Sky Sports, Coleman reflects: 'It was a big change and a massive step up for me. I found it difficult but as time passed I felt more comfortable and never looked back.'

Coleman, however, had to bide his time with Sligo and in his first season was a bit-part player. Because of his current standing in the game, that seems almost ridiculous. But his experience in Sligo, waiting for a chance to nail down a regular first-team role, should serve as an inspiration to young players in the league. When he eventually rubber-stamped a place in the side, making over 50 league appearances for The Showgrounds side, his swashbuckling style drew attention from Birmingham City, Celtic and West Ham United, as he remembers in an interview with *The Irish Times*.

'I did quite well at Celtic [on trial]. I don't know if Celtic and Sligo spoke about a transfer fee. Gordon Strachan was the manager. There was a trial game and I trained with the first team a couple of times and he took the training. I got word that they were interested to make something happen but I don't know how far it got. At Burnley I did quite well in training but I had a trial game and was injured after ten minutes. I was out for six weeks. So that never got going.

'Owen Coyle was the manager and was brilliant with me and looked after me, a gentleman. I went to Birmingham under Alex McLeish and I didn't really do great. It's hard going on trial. If I was Alex McLeish looking at me that week, I probably wouldn't have signed me either. On trial you're trying to do too much. It's difficult. Thankfully Everton didn't want me on trial. They just signed me,' he says.

Indeed they did. The Toffees, then managed by David Moyes, signed the 20-year-old for the sum of €60,000.

'It was strange and I couldn't believe Everton wanted to sign me,' he tells Sky Sports.

'There was part of me worried about leaving home for the first time. I signed a two-year contract and I looked at it as a two-year trial, really. And thankfully I was given a chance in the team,' he adds.

Since making his Everton debut in 2009, Coleman has played in over 200 Premier League games and is now regarded as one of the top defenders in England. For him, teenagers who move to English football are always going to find it difficult.

'It's tricky. Because I played in it, I am a big believer in the League of Ireland. There are some top players and some top clubs in it. But again, if Manchester United come in for you at 17? I love it over here now and I'm settled but I missed home a lot. I went over at 20 and I struggled. If I had to do it at 15 or 16, I'd have struggled massively. I try my best with all the young Irish lads here [at Everton] to make them feel at home but you're only with them for those two or three hours in the morning. They go back to their digs in the afternoon. There could be things they're missing at home. But then you're not going to turn down a Premier League club at 15 or 16. It's difficult because the League of Ireland was amazing, for me, it helped me get where I am today. That's the good part of it. But if you're 17 and Everton want to sign you, do you take a chance and say you'll play two more years in the League of Ireland and miss the boat?' says Coleman.

He is correct. That type of life-defining decision is very difficult for young players. In truth, they are not ready to make such big decisions at 16 and 17. And that's where they need proper guidance from their local clubs, coaches and their parents/guardians. Whether or not they are prepared to gamble by staying in Ireland for an extra couple of seasons, learning the trade and getting more ready for England, is up to them. But if you look at Coleman's example, and that of players like Kevin Doyle and Shane Long, who came through the League of Ireland and eventually became Premier League and international players, then it's clearly evident that there is another way forward.

And then there's Andy Boyle and Daryl Horgan, who starred for Dundalk in recent years and moved to England, together, in 2017. They also forced their way into the Republic of Ireland squad and Horgan, in particular, is tipped for a move to the Premier League in the future. I would say that their unbelievable fortunes in the last year or so – and also the impact of former St Patrick's Athletic midfielder Chris Forrester for Peterborough United – has given inspiration and hope to League of Ireland players that they can still make it to England.

Horgan (25) is the more naturally gifted of the two; a wide attacker capable of operating on either flank and most adept playing from the left, allowing him to cut inside to his more favoured right foot. He has experience, too, of playing from a more central position; of probing and trying to pick holes in opposition defences but to date the bulk of his best work has been done from the wings.

His form in helping Dundalk to three consecutive League of Ireland titles was nothing short of outstanding, earning many admirers at home and abroad. Indeed, the consistency and sharpness of his displays was so impressive that countless times before an eventual call-up to the Irish senior squad, many observers wondered why he was overlooked for some time by Martin O'Neill, who admirably kept tabs on his progress by attending many Dundalk matches, thus giving encouragement to domestic players that if they impress enough, O'Neill remains open about calling on League of Ireland players (unlike predecessor Giovanni Trapattoni, who paid scant regard to the domestic league).

There then came a point when O'Neill decided he could not continue to ignore Horgan's magical performances for the so-called Lilywhites. And along with Boyle, he was drafted into the Ireland squad for a World Cup qualifier against Austria.

Perhaps Horgan's cause was aided when his name was linked to a host of British clubs including Newcastle United. But aside from that, it was his natural ability – seen to perfection when Dundalk came close to becoming the first ever Irish team to reach the Champions League group stage before almost qualifying from their group in the Europa League – that proved to O'Neill and a host of others that Horgan was, in fact, the real deal capable of competing productively against more experienced and recognised players.

Yet, for Horgan to properly hone the talent developed in the youth ranks at Salthill Devon (in County Galway), he had to take some brave decisions in his early career.

Traditionally (or maybe habitually is a finer way of putting it) domestic Irish players tend to represent clubs in their geographic region. For example, players like

Horgan, from the west, normally play for teams such as Galway United and Sligo Rovers.

They might go as far as the midland region or sometimes to nearby Limerick. But rarely does a Galwegian, like Horgan, venture down south to Cork City, where Horgan's career sparked into life, after a season in the second tier with Salthill Devon.

He had experienced a rather uneventful short stay in the top division with Sligo Rovers, where current Wigan Athletic manager Paul Cook signed him, but was prepared to explore a path unfamiliar for westerners when agreeing to join Cork (on loan), and their battle to get out of the second tier after off-field problems led to demotion for breaching financial rules.

For sure, he could have taken the easy option by staying in the top flight with Sligo and playing a bit-part role. But instead he showed the desire to play week in and week out and it didn't seem to matter if that required a relinquishing of his status as a Premier Division player.

There, Horgan contributed heavily to Cork's First Division title win, leading to a permanent contract at Turners Cross. And over the next two seasons Horgan was instrumental in consolidating City's place back in the Premier Division. He developed rapidly in the Rebel County with Cork boss Tommy Dunne getting the very best from him, thereby turning his exciting but largely unproven potential into consistent productivity, and the passionate Cork supporters really took Horgan to their hearts.

However, in the pursuit of honours and European recognition, he eventually signed for ambitious Dundalk ahead of the 2014 season, having had trials with Barnsley and Torquay United in the Irish off-season.

And if one thought that Horgan might have peaked at Cork, they were mistaken. For it was with Dundalk, where manager Stephen Kenny (once of Dunfermline Athletic in Scotland), completely transformed the club, that Horgan's class really came to the fore. In his debut season he won the PFAI Young Player of the Year, as Dundalk won the League and League Cup. A League and FAI Cup (the country's most important cup competition) followed in 2015 before a hat-trick of league titles was sealed in 2016.

All the while, Horgan was showing great flair, accuracy from set pieces and the ability to score and assist, and when Dundalk faced more fearsome opponents in Europe, Horgan never shied away from the challenge and often led the Lilywhites to produce performances that some people felt beyond their ability.

For example, his goal in Dundalk's Europa League tie away against Zenit St Petersburg was a real classy effort, as he showed speed, awareness and composure when breaking through on goal from a long way out. Otherwise, Horgan is full of incisive and clever movement and his passing and short, sharp bursts of action are laced with conviction and genuine intent to hurt the opposition.

He has never been a winger to wait for the ball. Instead, he makes it happen by drifting into areas where he can influence matters, while also showing the right discipline and tactical acumen to know when and how to do so. His assured manner in possession, coupled with a head-down, hard-grafting attitude not always instilled in creative wingers, meant that a transfer to England was probably always going to be the next big step in Horgan's development and the inevitable move finally happened in 2017 when he signed for Preston North End.

And in his mid-20s, it looks like Horgan has not only chosen a perfect time to take the big step, but also selected a club that seem prepared to provide ample playing time to showcase his talent. Remember, his former Dundalk team-mates Pat Hoban and Richie Towell – both crucial players for the Lilywhites before signing for Oxford United and Brighton respectively – struggled to make an impact after crossing the water.

Indeed, Towell's fall from grace – going from the massive stand-out player in the League of Ireland to not even making Chris Hughton's matchday squad – has been pretty astounding, and his career, having looked so promising back home, has stalled completely since leaving Oriel Park.

So, picking the right club was always going to be one of Horgan's greatest challenges and after impressing greatly on his first league start – tormenting Brighton for much of the game and setting up Preston's second goal in a fine 2-0 win (in front of watching Irish assistant manager Roy Keane) – Horgan has since earned the complete trust of manager Simon Grayson; a really massive thing for an Irish player to acquire in the teething stages of an English adventure.

The Preston boss, who has also managed Huddersfield Town and Leeds United in recent years, also slowly integrated Boyle into the side and, having turned down advances from several English clubs in his teens in favour of getting a proper education, it is wonderful seeing Boyle fulfil his potential in England.

Like Horgan, a lot of Boyle's career was spent grafting and learning his trade in Irish football's semi-professional second tier before moving to Dundalk for the 2013 season. From there, he picked up three league titles and two domestic cups, as well as captaining Dundalk many times. And although his rise to English and international football was not as predicted as Horgan's, Boyle appears to have the heart, determination and positional sense to make a positive long-term impression at Deepdale, where fellow Irishmen Alan Browne, Greg Cunningham and Aiden McGeady (on loan from Everton) featured for the club in the 2016/17 season (Browne having also come through the League of Ireland with Cork City).

'These guys [Boyle and Horgan] have done it in the Europa League, in the Champions League when they've played against top opposition,' Simon Grayson told RTE's *Off the Ball* show.

'When I got a chance to meet them I was really impressed by their attitude and their hunger to succeed and ultimately we had to fight off quite a bit of competition for both players. The one thing I could do with both players is work with them and give them an opportunity in the Championship and see where their career goes from there,' he adds.

Like Coleman, Doyle and Long, they served their time in the League of Ireland and, most likely, learned an enormous amount there, before eventually moving to England when the time seemed right.

You won't convince parents/guardians that the League of Ireland is the place to be just because more nimble and technically assured players are gracing its playing fields. For sure, they will need more convincing. But what more needs to be said after analysing the careers of Boyle, Coleman, Doyle, Horgan and Long? They showed that great things can arise from shining in the League of Ireland. And perhaps if more people forget about the potential lucrative rewards of playing in England, and just settle for gentle progress for a while, they will reap the benefits later on.

Paul Osam, a former League of Ireland title winner and father to one of the domestic game's most promising players (Evan Osam), believes that more Irish players should consider this route to potential stardom.

'I think that Evan and every other Irish kid is better off staying here because you only really know if you're good enough for England after you reach 18 or 19,' he says.

'So, why not stay here to learn your trade at a very good level? You are learning from some very good coaches and playing in competitive matches every week. That's really how you find out about yourself, as a player. I feel there's just too much at stake for youngsters if they go to England in their mid-teens. I mean, you're away from home and family and friends, you go over unsure about the level of attention and coaching you will get, and your education suffers massively. I wouldn't endorse that sort of thing for my own son, or for any other young boy,' adds Osam, who believes Irish clubs are now developing much better technical players.

'We know that almost everyone wants to play in the Premier League and the Champions League. But it's just so hard to break into top level teams because they are world selections now. Then, our lads are broken-hearted when they return. You see squads in England and there's such an overload of players in certain positions, so it's hardly surprising when our kids don't get chances. But lately, a lot more kids are focusing on getting an education before going over and I think the new underage structures in the League of Ireland show the emphasis in this country, and in the league, is to improve things for our young players,' he says.

But what else can be done differently? What can young players do, if they are determined to try football abroad?

Well, instead of bemoaning the number of non-British players in English football, maybe the Irish can take a new route by looking into signing for clubs in other European countries. Places where there's a better chance of getting first-team opportunities, perhaps in Belgium and Holland, and where, unlike in England, the emphasis is on promoting young players into the first team.

These are other ways to the top and the sooner our young players are educated on this, the better for everyone involved. In Holland, for example, they provide great opportunities to play first-team football from a young age. Dublin-born Jack Byrne tried Dutch football for a loan spell in the 2015/16 season having found it impossible to break into the Manchester City side. There, he played almost 30 league matches in the Dutch top flight, providing him player with invaluable experience by playing against huge teams like Ajax, Feyenoord and PSV.

I genuinely feel that plenty of young Irish players should start looking at such options. In England, young players are up against such stiff competition from all over the world. And Alan Kirby, who spent four years at Aston Villa having joined as a promising 16-year-old, provides evidence of just how tough it can be.

A right-winger, Kirby excelled with Johnville in his native Waterford and won international honours with Ireland from Under-16 to Under-21 levels. He was a member of the Under-20 team to win bronze at the 1997 FIFA World Youth Championships and joined Villa in 1994. But he never played in the first team.

'If you manage to make the breakthrough and get a run of games you can build a reputation that can stand to you when looking for moves. But to stay as a seasoned professional in the Premier League takes incredible luck and in my opinion it's more likely to happen for defenders, rather than midfielders and attackers, in the modern game.

'On the pitch you have to be hungry, fit, fast, sharp and strong. Off the pitch you're expected to have a reserved social life – more girlfriend and cinema than nights out. I never really expected to get in the first team, although I mixed with them and occasionally trained. Aston Villa had a very good Premier League side. But look, they might as well have been Barcelona because I was a world away from ever starting a game. Villa had a large first-team squad and though I knew that they rated me, I wasn't going to get in front of the numerous million-pound midfielders who were either playing or sitting on the bench every week,' says Kirby.

'I always advise young Irish players, no matter who they are or what clubs they play for, to have a good plan B. If they're lucky enough to get to England, then study in the evening. And without sounding bitter or pessimistic, they should look at the statistics and realise that the English experience is going to end sooner than they'd like,' adds Kirby, who eventually returned home and became a four-time FAI Cup winner.

Of course, the odd Irish player will continue to squeeze their way into the plans of Premier League clubs. But it is happening less and less, and perhaps it is time for our young players to start carefully considering different options.

Then again, people are asking whether the impact of the UK leaving the European Union will affect the situation. Personally, I cannot see it making a huge difference to the fortunes of home-based players. Football, in my opinion, is worth so much money to the British economy that the clubs and people in positions of power (in the game and politically) will do whatever it takes to ensure that the impact of Brexit will be minimal for the English game and its mightily powerful Premier League elite.

At the time of writing, Premier League clubs were already pleading with the government to explore measures to protect the competition from the UK's impending departure from the European Union.

'The Premier League is the greatest league the world has ever known,' says the West Ham United co-chairman David Gold.

'It's a fantastic advert for Britain, for England. I know people talk about the wealth that's there, but the players are on huge salaries and all the tax is going into the exchequer. Why would you stifle that? Why would you want that to change? The Premier League goes around the world and it's ever-expanding. I don't see a government doing something potty to disturb that. I don't know about free movement but the structure would be that the best players would receive work permits,' Gold adds.

Tellingly, for me, the Stoke City owner Peter Coates said (in March 2017) that 'hopefully football will find a way of looking after itself'. Indeed, it usually does. And further, it's usually the massive clubs in the Premier League who get exactly what they want. In the case of Brexit, I don't expect sweeping changes and tons of home-based players to suddenly flood the playing fields. For the top clubs, I feel, will find ways around the potential difficulties that Brexit and the fall in the value of the pound could pose to continuing to attract the best foreign players from around the world. What those ways will be is anyone's guess. But money makes the game go around, and they will do everything in their power to protect themselves and their money-making machines no matter what outside influences, like Brexit, might pose to their continuing success.

Many people could disagree with this view. But I really don't see Premier League clubs allowing anything to stand in the way of making profits and building the most powerful teams that they can buy. This, of course, spells bad news for the future of Irish players in England. Indeed, for a country that once had it all, in terms of players lifting trophies for the best English sides, the future looks far from spectacular. It looks a bit like a closed shop now. The foreign players and managers have taken over. And the home-based players are banging on the window trying to get in. But the shutters are coming down, gradually. And they might never open again.